Christian and Wholeness

AN APPROACH TO CHRISTIAN HEALING

Dame Raphael Frost, OSB

C

JAMES CLARKE & CO
Cambridge

British Library Cataloguing in Publication Data

Frost, Evelyn
  Christ and wholeness: the integral relationship
  between wholeness and Christian renewal.
  1. Spiritual healing
  I. Title
  615.8'52   BT732.5

  ISBN 0–227–67888–5

First published in 1985 by
James Clarke & Co., Ltd
7 All Saints' Passage
Cambridge CB2 3LS

Photoset and printed in Great Britain by
Redwood Burn Limited, Trowbridge, Wiltshire

Contents

Foreword by Bishop Morris Maddocks

I owe my early interest in the Church's ministry of healing to the late Dr Henry Cooper who was my first vicar. For me, he personified the Guild of S. Raphael with its sound sacramental teaching. He devotedly edited its publication – *Chrism* – for tens of years. He it was who gave me Evelyn (Dame Raphael) Frost's *Christian Healing*. I am delighted that James Clarke and Co. are now publishing this posthumous work of hers.

As a Christian, Dame Raphael was possessed by the fruits of Christ's victory in his cross and resurrection. Her heart beat with the rhythm of the early Christians. She was in tune with *Christ and Wholeness*, the title given to this last testament to her faith.

When I read her quotation from that great chaplain of Christ's, Cambridge at the turn of the century, Forbes Robinson, I felt the words originally spoken to ordinands in Winchester Cathedral told of what she succeeded in being:

> You yourself must be the proof that the resurrection has taken place, that Christ is alive . . . The average man does not know what Christianity is: you must reveal it to him. You must show him . . . what it can do for a human being . . . Live Christ before his eyes.

In these pages, Dr Evelyn Frost shows what the healing gospel of the risen Christ can do for a human being, how it is effective in bringing about that health and salvation, that wholeness of personality, that is God's will for man, created in his own image. 'For the Christian,' she writes, 'living in line with the purpose of creation and abiding in Christ and Christ in him, there is a wholeness of body, mind and spirit that is strong to resist the onslaught of disease and ride the storms and tensions of life in a special way.' Here is a breath of fresh air, a glimpse of the spring-time of the Early Church which the healing movement has constantly sought to bring before the consciousness of the Church in this century. It is thanks to such people as Dame Raphael that this fresh air of 'being' is blowing with increasing vigour on the airless activism of a 'doing' church. How interesting (for instance) her comment on Christian stewardship: strict tithing would include a rule of two and a half hours prayer each day!

The healing dimension is being given back to the Church in our time. For this bounty, we can only praise God. Dame Raphael's scholarship has here brought out the highlights of this dimension in the Church's history, both in the writings of the Fathers and in the lives of the Saints. Like all prophets, she was concerned with the Church of the present and the future. Her historical research showed her that the secret of being a healing church lay in the depths of its spiritual life. Can we learn from this essay on Christ and Wholeness that the ministry of healing must grow from within the life of our contemporary Church, that it must be the reflection and expression of the Church's inner life? For just as the wholeness a Christian seeks is a healing of his inner being in Christ, so the health of a Church will depend on the wholeness of its life of prayer. A Church with a strong inner life, with a devoted purpose of being in Christ, will be a healing Church, for it will communicate to mankind 'Christ and Wholeness'. Let us be grateful that the author has helped us to see this.

Preface and acknowledgements

This book has been written in response to many requests from those who have read previous writings of mine, and especially *Christian Healing: A Consideration of the Place of Spiritual Healing in the Church of Today in the Light of the Doctrine and Practice of the Ante-Nicene Church.**

It is written for the ordinary reader, clerical or lay, who has no time for specialized research in this subject. For the benefit of any who wish to study at greater length I have added details in chapter notes and references in the text, and the appendix on pages 95–100.

I have attempted to clarify the distinctively Christian approach, not as a theology of healing, but by seeing healing as an integral part of Christian theology. I have considered how this was first presented and how it can be re-presented today.

Unless otherwise noted, the scripture references are taken from the Jerusalem Bible.

My thanks are due to the Guild of S. Raphael for permission to use some of the material from articles I wrote originally for their quarterly magazine, also to F. Lovsky, author of *L'Eglise et les malades – depuis le IIe Siècle jusqu'au début du XXe Siècle*, particularly for details relative to developments in some of the post-reformation churches.

Evelyn Frost
(Dame Raphael Frost OSB)
Burford, Oxford

---

* Now out of print after three editions.

A note on the author

When, in 1950, Dr Evelyn Frost exchanged a distinguished academic career and a fruitful pastorate in Christian teaching and healing for life in an enclosed religious community, many of those who knew her must have been surprised, some even saddened. She herself, however, responded to God's call with characteristic courage, in spite of the difficulties inevitably encountered in a 'late vocation'. How great was the blessing granted to Dame Raphael (for such was her name in the Anglican Benedictine community of which she became a member) in her new life could not be better demonstrated than in this, her final work. As a nun, she was indeed 'truly possessed by the fruits of Christ's victory in his cross and resurrection'.

It is surely significant that the ideal of the Benedictine life which is the background of this book is that same 'wholeness' to which we are directed in its title. Benedict saw this primarily as a directive for the individual monk or nun. He sets it, however, in the wider context of that stability and peace which should be the hallmark of every Benedictine community and through which they contribute to the healing of divisions and to the restoration of wholeness in the Church. As a nun in the 'school of the Lord's service' at Burford, Dame Raphael made these great themes her own, while her own apostolate of prayer was enriched by the liturgical life of her Community as it is expressed in the daily Eucharist and in the monastic office.

In monastic tradition the means of gaining such stability has always been through a balanced life of prayer, manual work and study, but, in this age of scarce vocations, this has become an ideal rarely enjoyed by most religious. In this, Dame Raphael was no exception, and it is a measure of her achievement and of her mature and disciplined intellect that much of this book was researched and written in those odd moments which make up the 'intervals' of the monastic day.

Finally, there remains one aspect of Dame Raphael's life which is fundamental to any true assessment of her work. For, in the latter years of her life, she struggled against the increasing handicap of arthritis and a daily crucifixion of intense pain. To probe into God's deep purposes during these years would, one feels, be an impertinence, and Dame Raphael would surely have preferred to be remembered for that brand of humour which is so often the mark of the mature Christian character. Nowhere was this more apparent than in her attitude to a wheelchair which, often adorned with various gadgets and 'aids', frequently of her own invention, she regarded not as an end to active living but as a welcome extension of it.

Thus, *Christ and Wholeness* is truly a testimonial 'written in flesh and blood' and there can be no better proof than Dame Raphael's own life 'that the resurrection has taken place, that Christ is alive'.

Introduction – The Challenge

The present drawing together of Christians through the ecumenical movement, the impact of other faiths through modern means of communication, together with the widespread development in scientific research means that those responsible for work in medical, social, pastoral and educational spheres will meet with a wide variety of healing ministries; good, bad or indifferent, many of which claim religious credentials. Amidst the labyrinth of differing, sometimes conflicting, teaching and practice there is need for a clarification of the essentially Christian approach, more particularly because many are being lost to the Church by turning to all kinds of cults that claim healing power.

Several years ago, for example, a schoolgirl who took her religion very seriously after her confirmation in the Church of England remarked: 'Christ commanded us to preach the Gospel and heal the sick; I do not see the sick being healed', and she left the Church to become a Christian Scientist. This is no isolated instance, and challenges us to examine how far the Church is fulfilling her healing ministry today, and what still remains to be done.

This challenge raises the following questions: What is unique about the Christian contribution? Does it differ in kind or only in degree from what is possible to the non-Christian? Is it understood by those both within and outside the Church? Is due attention being given to it by those who represent the Church in their welcome cooperation with other healing ministries, and by those who write about the Church's ministry of healing?

To answer these questions, both current circumstances and original doctrine and practice need to be considered in order to

1

recognise what is essential, and to evaluate the presentation of the Christian ministry of healing today.

In the early centuries healing was a marked feature of the life and witness of the Church. During the ensuing centuries many factors tended to obscure or falsify this early teaching. One of the difficulties has been due to the understandable reluctance to discard the outdated language in which these truths were presented. It may not be possible to reclothe them in modern dress; fashions of thought and terminology as well as of clothing change so rapidly. Throughout the centuries, contemporary ideas and associations have, sometimes misleadingly, expressed them in varied figurative language in accordance with the insights of the time. Whilst fundamental truths must endure, there is much in the manner of presentation and still more in practical application that may need to be discarded or changed. At present, there is no commonly accepted terminology which is both accurate and unambiguous, although some valuable work in this direction has been done by Teilhard de Chardin, among others. The efforts of the early Church to find exact Latin or Greek terminology for accuracy of expression illustrates the delicate and difficult task of translation into any language. Differences of interpretation have led to errors and misunderstandings, whilst in addition there has been credulity, superstition and crude forms of practice. The rapid developments of science and technology have had their own repercussions; at certain periods of history the relations between the Church and the medical profession have been strained. In the days of Deism, many types of healing now easily explicable were indiscriminately rejected as magic or superstition.

Developments in the scientific field and the welcome increase in priest–doctor co-operation are factors which call for a re-presentation of the theological position freed from the errors and misunderstandings that have led to estrangement in the past, and also for a sifting of the theology of healing from the transitory accretions which have grown up in connection with it.

Trends of modern life and thought have to be considered as a background to the reappraisal of Christian healing. Christian healing has to be examined at its source, namely in the doctrine and practice of the primitive church and its development in these early centuries. For this essential task there is abundant material both in the New Testament and in the other writings of the ante-Nicene Church. This will define the 'why' and the 'how' for the present day.

It will then be necessary to make a brief survey of subsequent history to see in what directions there has been misunderstanding of, or a deviation from, the original; this will clear the way for a consideration of the present position, examining what has already been achieved and what is needed for a fuller and more effective restoration of the healing ministry of the Church.

Although volumes could be written on these various aspects of the subject, sufficient can be said in a small compass to indicate how, in the context of the modern world, this restoration can be effected in line with the teaching which the apostles were the first custodians of.

Part 1

1

Aspects of the modern background in relation to health and disease

Wholeness

In modern scientific thought the diagnosis and treatment of disease places the physical in the context of the psychological and social. This corroborates what has been implicit in the Christian approach to healing from the first. Although such terms as psychosomatic or holistic were not known, what they signified was not only present but essential to the Christian gospel. The Greek phraseology of body, mind and spirit was used, but it was man in his wholeness, not some isolated component termed 'soul' or 'spirit', who was redeemed.

Before the days of modern psychology, S. Paul was exhorting his readers to fill their minds with 'everything that is true, everything that we love and honour, and everything that can be thought virtuous and worthy of praise'.[1] He saw the connection between spiritual and physical health.

The New Testament is full of this, not because sin is a breaking of commands, but because those commands define the conditions for the well-being both of society and the individual; they represent a clear insight into the nature of man and how it can best find fulfilment; thus to deviate from them is to suffer loss. Today the connection is known in a psychosomatic context; for example the connection between resentment or anxiety and certain physical conditions.

The recognition of the factors of heredity, the contemporary environment and the whole past history of the race, part of which Carl Jung, the Swiss psychologist saw as constituting 'the collective unconscious' of an individual, throws light not only on diagnosis and treatment but also on the traditional language of sin and guilt and the tremendous healing power of the Incarnation, bringing the fullness of divine life into the life-stream of the human race, a life mediated through the Holy Spirit in the Church which is His Body on Earth.

It is beyond the power of science, however far advanced, to see the whole man in true proportion. Life can be prolonged by many modern techniques, including spare-part transplants, psychological problems can be more effectively dealt with than in the past, but man is neither a disembodied spirit nor something that can be created by a combination of psychology and technical skills – all that the test tube may be able to do is to reproduce; even as the life is in the seed, so the fundamental principles of human nature are already present. When one speaks of the wholeness of man this is more than to speak of the spare parts into which analysis can dissect him.

> What a piece of work is man! How noble in person! How infinite in faculty! in form, in moving, how express and admirable! in action like an angel! in apprehension how like a god! the beauty of the world! the paragon of animals.[2]

In addition to emotion, intellect and will, human personality has a spiritual nature. This has sometimes been called a 'God hunger', i.e. a sense of the infinite – 'Our hearts are restless till they rest in Thee',[3] a restlessness very evident in the present day. For this reason Christian healing has a vital part to play in cooperation with other skills for the wholeness of man. In the entirety of both his present and his potential personality man is known only to his creator. Christ came to make men whole.

All consideration of the Christian healing ministry today must be seen within this wider context, for it is not the removal of symptoms that is in question, but the healing of the whole person.

Evolution

In a materialistic age and a permissive society, a reappraisal of the real meaning of progress is vital to the well-being of both the individual and the race.

Long before the days of Darwin, probably the best exposition of the goal of evolution was made by S. Paul when he wrote: 'Creation still retains the hope of being freed, like us, from its slavery to decadence to enjoy the same freedom and glory as the children of God. From the beginning until now the entire creation, as we know, has been groaning in one great act of giving birth.'[4] He did not know the long process of evolution now known in greater detail, but his insight into the direction in which it moves was profound.

A backward look at the factors that make man what he is shows a movement which cannot be regarded as a completed process; still greater heights lie ahead. If the end to which this process is moving can be recognized it will give purpose and direction to the present. The oak tree tells us more of its nature than the acorn.

Signposts to this are the characteristics which have already emerged, such as the power to make conceptual inferences and a capacity to become free from total involvement in the world in order to advance still further. These represent a degree of freedom over the lower nature from which man has emerged and some element of self-determination by intellect and responsible direction of the will.

It can be seen that to drift into the animal level, undirected by man's higher faculties is a retrograde step, unsuitable and unworthy of the dignity of human nature, whose freedom is not license but designed with a view to further evolutionary progress, to retard which is injurious both to the individual and to the well-being of the race.

There are those, moreover, who press on to higher things, and amongst human values are to be found love, self-sacrifice, truth, beauty and goodness (to which the Christian would add the less understood values of humility and meekness); qualities of mature human character; those possessing them to any marked degree are honoured and admired, for they are fine specimens of humanity.

Emergence on to the next stage necessarily means an advance beyond the known, but these signposts indicate something to be measured by spiritual rather than physical values. The experience of 'the weakest to the wall' as a natural law would in this case mean the weakest not physically, but in character conform-

able to the end to which man is emerging. The survival of the fit-
test is not that of a glorified animal but of the highest
development of which man is capable. To slip back or to advance
are live alternatives affecting the health of the individual or race;
'the wages of sin is death', the lesser manifestations of which can
be seen in disease and disharmony – any newspaper shows this
to be the case!

Man in his process of transition has the expanding consciousness of 'the Beyond that is within'. There is a spiritual restlessness analogous to that of nature in springtime, a pressing on to a
more mature development, a restlessness which theology would
ascribe to the fact that man not only comes from God but is
destined for God; this confronts him with a challenge to respond
to the inner pressure, and to advance.

The Christian speaks of a new nature, of yet another factor
introduced into the life of man, not by evolution but by the incarnation of Christ, raising him by regeneration to membership of
the Body of Christ, which is a divinization of man, leading him to
a yet greater goal. In this new nature are laws not so readily
applicable to the old; what to the latter seem miracles may have a
'natural' place here.

If this regenerate life throws light on the way ahead, if this is
the way of progress, life according to its laws will give harmony
and thus health and wholeness to man, as well as meaning and
direction to the present. Such laws are shown by the life, death
and resurrection of Christ to be not legalistic codes but basically
the law of love calling for self-sacrifice, of life through death.

Since it is to the attainment of man's potential that he must
ever strive and not just drift with the tide, it is vital to his well-
being to press forward; and it is Christ who claims to be the way,
the truth and the life by which mankind in him may attain the
goal, until, as S. Paul expresses it: 'We become the perfect Man,
fully mature with the fullness of Christ himself'.[5]

Technology

The harnessing of electricity so that life may be seen on the
coloured television screen, the recapturing of past events by the
computer, the preservation of sound by the tape recorder, or
even voices heard from the moon; all these point to the fact that

far different forms are now needed for the measurement and description of what was formerly known as solid matter.

The mysterious universe as it unfolds its secrets reveals marvels behind the electron, and possibly the ultimate discovery in that research may be to do with the personality.

The materialism of the past has gone and it is recognized that new categories which include imponderables are needed; nor can 'matter' be isolated from a context with which there is inevitable interaction, an interaction which includes extra-sensory factors. All this throws light on the subject of miracles. It demonstrates that it is both unreasonable and unscientific to reject as impossible, the inexplicable. On the subject of healing this forbids the unqualified use of the term 'incurable'; already with the knowledge of penicillin, radiotherapy, etc., the range of what was formerly termed 'incurable' has been considerably lessened. All the specialist can say with any degree of truth would be that in his own field of research he does not yet know of a cure. Today something beyond our natural experience is classed as a miracle, tomorrow the explanation may be found. However, if truth is infinite there will always be that which is beyond the horizon of our finite minds and thus always a place for revelation and the corresponding effect of faith operating in the light of revelation.

In spite of all the advantages of technology there are dangers affecting health; some of these are:

1. A feeling of self-sufficiency. With the great expansion of knowledge there is the danger of thinking in terms of a man-made universe, and seeking to mould revelation to fit acquired knowledge.
2. Fear. Because of the resources at man's disposal there is fear of the consequences of misuse; the term 'cold war', the cause of much neurosis, has come into use with the increasing knowledge of such things as nuclear fission, radioactive matter, etc.
3. Depersonalization. In the olden days of craft guilds people could find their interest in their creative work. This has now been replaced by mechanisms; man finds himself working on a conveyor belt instead of at a craft, and his individuality is eclipsed, or he becomes an impersonal 'hand', liable to redundancy and needing to find his interests outside working hours.

4. Unproductive leisure. Manual working hours now lessened by technical devices give leisure for healthy development, but there is danger of such opportunity being misused.

This is not by any means to disparage the magnificent, dedicated work of so many researching in this way, nor the very great contribution to the healing and prevention of disease that has resulted from their labours. Nevertheless, it is an open question whether, in general, man has reached a sufficient degree of maturity to be trusted with so much technical skill, or whether he is so infantile as to turn it to selfish ends, to aggression and ultimately self-destruction. In so far as the latter is the case, disease and destruction are the inevitable consequences.

To counteract these dangers there is need for a sense of balance and proportion. There are limits to human knowledge; such knowledge needs to be adapted to revelation and not vice versa. It is only in the context of revealed truth that all knowledge finds its place. Only with a view to the purpose and direction to which the universe is designed can such knowledge serve any real constructive purpose.

Insight into this can bring harmony, peace, healing and strength. This is the place for worship, and in this context the universe can be brought more into line with the original design for which it was created, and over which man was placed as custodian. It is how mankind can find health and healing through the harmonious working of his environment. At the present stage this may appear utopian; but it is a long-term plan towards which each successive generation has its contribution to make so that the salvation of mankind can be realized and for which the Christian believes Christ died, who within and through his followers continues his redeeming work.

Extra-sensory perception

Technology can never satisfy the craving of the human spirit. Instinctively, although not always consciously acknowledged, man feels for something deeper and more fundamental. It can hardly be surprising, therefore, that there is today a swing of the pendulum towards the extra-sensory and the exploration of various forms of preternatural experience. Many of these forms are attractive as a temporary escape from the rat-race of a materialistic age, from boredom and the pressures of insecurity; they also appeal to the innate curiosity of man. There is, therefore, the thoughtless, irresponsible resort to ESP alongside serious study and research and the groping enquiry for something to satisfy a need.

The wide range of ESP covers magnetic, telepathic and other phenomena. As with technology, so here the dawn of a scientific approach points to the danger of a too hasty judgement which either rejects evidence without examination, or accepts it without adequate grounds.

Today there is a Medical Society for the Study of Radionics, in the USA an Academy of Parapsychology and a Foundation for Parasensory Investigation, and some universities have a place for such study in their curriculum. Leading scientists have postulated that matter rests upon an unseen world of energy. Is the increasing investigation of the current of energy known as odic force an elementary insight into this?

It has long been recognized that there are people endued with extra-sensory perception, for example gypsies, 'sensitives', those with magnetic power or the power of telepathy. Like the perceptive power of normal senses such as sight or hearing, these faculties represent a special natural endowment which can be used for good or ill. In the past, men like Sir Kenelm Digby, Valentine Greatrakes, Mesmer, Gassner and others were known to produce beneficial results usually associated with healing. Their contemporaries did not know modern science and put their own interpretations, often connected with religion, on such experiences. Very special responsibility rests upon people so endowed not to open doors to forces injurious to themselves and others, for the temptation to do so will be greater for them than for those less sensitive in these ways; on the other hand they possess latent powers which can be used for good.

Greater scientific knowledge is finding a possible further method of healing along these lines. In the generations to come research in this field may open up ways of healing which may dominate other healing disciplines. The study of radionics is already pointing in this direction but at the present stage, whilst there are those who may be acting from the best motives, this same knowledge can be used for very harmful ends, as can already be recognized from the evils resulting from a knowledge

of the technique of brainwashing. When those working for healing open their personalities to act as spiritualist mediums the
devil can disguise himself as an angel of light and do untold
harm.

Our scientific laws are always needing modification or recast-
ing in the light of fresh knowledge; in the meantime, for those
who are not specializing in scientific research in ESP, to work
upon the human aura, or to try to manipulate the etheric body by
trance or other media could be more highly dangerous than to release the knowledge of nuclear fission to the man in the street.

There is abundant evidence to show that in this field there are
forces that militate against the health and well-being of man. The
door can be opened, especially in the psychic context, to forces
that may produce disastrous consequences beyond man's control; consequences affecting a wider range than the individual
immediately concerned. Many claims to healing through the
agency of spiritualist mediums can be classed in this category, as
can attempts to contact the departed by this means. One need
not go to the extreme of black magic or Satanism to realize it is no
idle phrase that speaks of 'giving place to the devil'. Much
derangement, spiritual, mental and physical, is known to have
been caused in this connection, even through such apparently
mild toying with the subject as table-turning, or the ouija board.
Doors can be opened, often unintentionally, to evils that cannot
easily be restrained. Schoolgirls, from curiosity or the desire to
be 'with it', have been led by the superficial appearance of harm-
lessness to a first step towards more dangerous experimentation
in the occult, with tragic consequences. There is here a real conflict between light and darkness, and the devil is quite used to
disguising himself in subtle and misleading ways.

Throughout history such practices have been well known, but
a scientific age has lent more credibility to them, and the widespread interest in this subject at the present time must be a
matter of concern for all engaged in Christian healing. Scripture
takes a strong hand in this respect: Isaiah condemned those who
'consult the mediums and the wizards who chirp and mutter'[6]
and the Jewish law condemned in the strongest terms the one
'who . . . practices divination, who is a soothsayer, augur or sor-
cerer, who uses charms, consults ghosts or spirits, or calls up the
dead';[7] for some of these practices the penalty was death.[8, 9]

In the New Testament the same strong line is taken,[10] whilst the story of Simon Magus[11] shows how clear cut the difference is between light and darkness. In the Gospels all the healing works of Christ are shown as the defeat of evil, whether bringing freedom from physical ills, death or demoniac forces.

This subject has been treated at some length because much at the present day that needs healing stems from this source, and it is important to diagnose the cause, and redirect man's quest into true channels of life and healing.[12]

Insecurity

Much has contributed during this century to a feeling of insecurity. There have been two world wars on an unprecedented scale including the horrors of atomic warfare; there are sporadic outbreaks of war in various parts of the world, and advances in technology have opened up still more terrifying prospects. Associated with all this is the cold war and uneasy relations between world powers.

In the social sphere the security of family life has been undermined; divorce, abortion and permissiveness have meant an insecure background for children, with all the anti-social and psychological disturbances that follow from it. Urbanization and the ease of international travel are factors which have changed the pattern of the closeknit family unit.

Inflation, fear of redundancy in work or bankruptcy in management, and general industrial unrest and the modern problems of housing all contribute to a general feeling of insecurity. This is all aggravated by widespread violence, hijacking, cold-blooded murder and other forms of crime.

It does not need much knowledge of psychology to see how all this militates against health. The paralysing effect of fear can weaken resistance and the will to live; it can produce the hopelessness leading to inertia or to the various forms of escapism such as alcoholism, drug addiction and many other situations that call for help from the Samaritans and other organizations designed to meet these needs.

Although there is a real call for Christian healing here, it is not only to cure or alleviate symptoms but rather to give the confidence and security that draws strength from a living, experimental faith in the concern of Divine Providence for each individual. There is also a call to eradicate the causes of these ills by a renewal of life in accordance with Christ's teaching, and in union with the person of Christ: for the man-made world needs to give place to the God-made world.

A search for meaning in religion

The search for meaning in religion has taken various forms, almost all of which have a positive contribution to make to healing.

Amongst the youth of today there is a violent reaction against the religious structures and institutions of former times; much to them appears irrelevant or meaningless and they are apt to associate the old Victorianism with hypocrisy and sentimentality. This leads them to demand a strict integrity in worship and worshippers. The decreasing interest in some quarters in organized religion is often due to dissatisfaction with what they find. The phrase 'God is dead' is not directed to the deity himself so much as to the unacceptable ways in which he has been presented. Amongst the young there is to be found a desire for reality and sincerity which is variously expressed.

One form of expression is in sacrificial service, sometimes based on humanism, sometimes profoundly Christian, for example voluntary service overseas, help and care for the aged, sponsored walks, etc.; whilst movements such as Moral Rearmament, the Festival of Light or the Jesus movement show a real concern for Christian witness in a permissive society.

Another very popular approach is in some form of contemplation. Eastern mysticism makes a great appeal and the practice of Yoga exercises are enthusiastically undertaken; the teachings of Buddhism and the Maharishi are followed, whilst within Christianity courses of contemplative meditation are being given. The fortunate few are discovering the great mystics such as S. John of the Cross or S. Teresa of Avila: there is need for much more guidance from the Church to help seekers to find these truly great mystics within her own borders.

Vatican II and the work of Pope John XXIII have led to widespread liturgical reform which should go far to meet the demand for relevant and meaningful worship. They have also inspired ecumenical ventures in both the social and religious fields, and fresh experiments in community life, including ecumenical communities, are being undertaken, for example at Taizé.

All these trends have a great contribution to make to healing. The humanitarian service, the witness to Christian moral standards, the relaxation practised in some systems of contemplation, the shared care and responsibility by ecumenical and other communities all contribute in their own way to the prevention or relief of disease.

One increasingly widespread influence can be seen in the Charismatic movement. In all renewal movements there are apt to be dangers of aberrations, but in so far as this movement represents a genuine witness to the power of the Holy Spirit released as in the days of the primitive church, the beneficial, healing effects can be immeasurably great, for there is no limit to the power of God operating through the Holy Spirit. The greatest healing benefits however are to be found not so much in the cure of disease, for which there is plenty of evidence, as in the reintegration of the personality with a true orientation of life, which issues in a wholeness both of the individual and of social relationships, and in healthy moral standards.

Chapter notes

1. Philippians 4. 8.
2. Shakespeare, *Hamlet*.
3. S. Augustine, *Confessions* I. 1.
4. Romans 8. 19–23.
5. Ephesians 4. 13.
6. Isaiah 8. 19 RSV.
7. Deuteronomy 18. 10.
8. Leviticus 20. 27.
9. See further Leviticus 20. 6; 19. 26, 31; Exodus 22. 18; Micah 5. 12; Malachi 3. 5 and the story of Saul's visit to the Witch of Endor, I Samuel 28.
10. See Galatians 5. 26; Revelation 21. 8; 22. 15; Acts 16. 16; 19. 19.
11. Acts 8. 9–24.
12. See further pp. 48ff. 81 (on exorcism).

Part 2

An outline history of Christian healing

1

The theological background

To appreciate the theology of Christian healing a necessary preliminary is a consideration of the use of the word 'salvation', since so many words have in the course of time lost some of their original overtones, for example the word 'sacrifice'. The word 'salvation', which with its derivatives features so prominently in the New Testament, occurring over one hundred times, is integral to the Gospel of Salvation, but has lost much of its connection with health. When used today in a religious context it is almost wholly associated with the spiritual aspect. This fails to do justice to the word in Greek, Latin and Syriac, where health and well-being are included in the root meaning of the word.

When the first translation of the New Testament into the vernacular was made, every time this word was used it was translated by 'health'.[1] With the help of a concordance much light can be thrown on the New Testament teaching on this subject by reading this word in place of the word 'salvation', for example: 'The scriptures are able to make thee wise unto health',[2] and 'the science of health to His people by the remission of sins.'[3]

The key to the understanding of Christian healing and its unique contribution to other methods of healing is the truth that Christ is our contemporary, at hand to heal and save, as in New Testament times. Christ, who in his days on earth healed all who came to him; who before his Ascension promised 'All authority in heaven and on earth has been given to me',[4] which authority is available now as then; whose will for the salvation of man both in body and soul has never altered, and who delegated his power to others.

It is easy to think of him as one who lived nearly two thousand years ago, of whom we have no biography, but a collection of reminiscences from those who knew and loved him at that time. The New Testament, however, gives more than an account of what he did and was during his earthly life. From the day of Pentecost onwards there is the presence of the risen, glorified Lord. It is experience of this Christ active in contemporary situations that underlies the healing recorded in the Acts. After Pentecost 'they ... preached everywhere, the Lord working with them, and confirming the word by the signs that accompanied it'.[5] S. Peter's account of the healing of the lame man at the Beautiful Gate of the Temple says, 'It is in the name of Jesus which, through our faith in it, has brought back the strength of this man'.[6] In the raising of Anaeas Peter said, 'Anaeas, Jesus Christ cures you'.[7]

Over and over again his ever-present activity is experienced. S. John who had known him in the days of his flesh now experiences his presence in a new dimension, through his Spirit. The Fourth Gospel indicates how his earthly life can be a signpost to this experience. S. Luke, S. Paul and other New Testament writers show what this signifies for them,[8] and this is true in the subsequent life and experience of the Church down to the present day.

He has many ways of healing. Throughout history there has been his healing mediated through all those who care for sufferers. His present activity can often be more directly realized with the help of some outward and visible sign such as a sacrament or a touch. These help the sufferer to appreciate both his presence and his will to heal; it is he and no other who is the healer.

Amongst the Jews a name was far more than a personal label, it embraced characteristics of the person and his function. Jesus came as saviour from sin and its consequences. 'The wages paid by sin are death',[9] i.e. the consequences of sin do not only affect man's soul but his whole being, including the physical. Enough is recorded of Jesus' incarnate life to leave no doubt about the physical part of his saving work; it clearly demonstrates that his healing ministry is part of the whole scheme of salvation through which man is redeemed, restored and directed to his fulfilment in God.

Christianity emphasizes two important truths about man's nature:

1. It is an integral whole and must be treated as such. Christ

came as the Saviour of the whole man, not of some component part only. The departmentalization of special disciplines in healing work has sometimes in the past obscured this, and so too at times in history has a rift between the Church and the medical profession.[10]

2. In essence it is wholly good, whatever foreign elements may have found their way into the lifestream. 'God created man in the image of himself.... God saw all he had made, and indeed it was very good'.[11] This stands out significantly in contrast to the largely dualistic philosophy of the pagan world into which Christianity came.

Disaster occurred when the creature–creator relationship was ignored. Not only are there laws known to science governing man's well-being which are ignored at his peril, but also the far more fundamental 'I–Thou' relationship with God. A profound truth is illustrated by the Garden of Eden story, when the self-assertiveness of man in disobedience to God was sufficient to throw the whole of human living out of gear. Deliberate disobedience, opposition to and defiance of God and the opposition to love bear fruit in aggression, cruelty, oppression, indifference to the claims of God and man; all of which are breeding-grounds for physical and mental ills. Added to that, because of the solidarity of mankind, the misuse by individuals of man's capacity to live by human and not sub-human standards involved the whole of mankind in a disastrous situation in which he was not only out of line with his true destiny, but often in direct opposition to it; this was intensified and augmented by each successive generation, and thus a toxic element was introduced into the lifestream. There is no standing still, failure to progress forward involves going backward.

Factors other than human ones also played their part in contributing to this situation. Man was not the only or first agent of disorder. There is good reason to recognize that 'It is not against human enemies that we have to struggle, but against the Sovereignties and the Powers who originate the darkness in this world, the spiritual army of evil'.[12] Experience, especially at the present time when so much attention is being drawn to the occult, bears this out.

The radical tragedy is that in this way the personal relationship of man with God, his true end, was injured or broken. The consequences of this was maladjustment in various forms, disharmony, disease and death. In the life of society these were manifest as war, oppression and other forms of social or international evil; in the life of the individual as physical, mental and spiritual ills.

In this situation humanity was incapable of healing itself unaided: when the laws of nature are broken nature takes its revenge. A counterbalancing contribution, if it could be made without violating the essential freedom of man, was the only solution. It was because evil is foreign to man's essential nature that there was no inherent obstacle to the Incarnation of the Saviour of the World. It was the union of the immortal with corrupted nature that was to destroy death. According to S. Irenaeus the object of the Incarnation was 'to join the end to the beginning, that is, man to God'[13] thus restoring to man what by the Fall he had lost. The Incarnation had a radical effect upon human nature, enabling man 'to share in the divinity of Christ, who humbled himself to share in our humanity'.[14]

In his divine and perfect life united with human nature Christ met the full force of evil, triumphing over it through obedience unto a real human death. His life, death and resurrection reveal the healing will of God, and through the operation of the Holy Spirit he brings man into vital contact with the life of God. He thus inaugurates a new phase of life for man, a life quickened by the Spirit through regeneration and incorporation into his Body, into which the believer normally enters by baptism. Through his Body the Spirit of God works the healing works of God.

The will of God to heal was seen throughout Christ's earthly mission, not only or primarily in the healing miracles, but in his teaching, calling men to care for the welfare of others, for example the parables of the Good Samaritan, Dives and Lazarus, the Prodigal Son, the Sheep and the Goats – to name only four. It is seen in his denunciation of the Pharisees, in fact throughout the whole Gospel story, culminating in his crucifixion for man's salvation.

This is in line with Old Testament teaching, especially according to the prophets. Love, justice and mercy are all characteristics of that outgoing, self-sacrificing love which by its very nature heals; Christ heals because he is the embodiment of this love, and now as then brings blessings which benefit the whole man, working through his Body the Church, which has been described as the extension of the Incarnation. It is a fallacy to leave physical healing out of the picture although this has frequently been done in the past; it is the whole man who benefits. This was so well known and appreciated in the early days of Christianity that healing was a normal function. The Acts of the Apostles and the other writings of the early Church are abundant evidence of this.[15]

In the regenerate life, normally entered at baptism, man goes forward to his true destiny, and restlessness and disillusionment are replaced by a sense of purpose and meaning. As this life develops the healing fruits of the Spirit are seen. Love, joy, peace and so on, are as 'natural' to the regenerate life as the fruit is to its native tree. Life in line with the purpose of creation spells harmony, poise and health, not only for the individual but flowing out in healing to mankind.

It is in the context of this new life that forces operate, not formulated by, nor opposed to the laws of the former life, but transcending them by reason of new factors.

It is only to be expected that as man progresses towards the climax of his development he will meet that for which his previous experience can provide no rational explanation. In the regenerate life laws may well be operative which may be called miraculous: 'The powers of the world to come'.[16] It would be unreasonable to expect anything different.

Chapter notes

1. Tyndale's first translation, 1525.
2. 2 Timothy 3. 15.
3. Luke 1. 77.
4. Matthew 28. 19.
5. Mark 16. 20.
6. Acts 3. 16; see also 4. 9, 10.
7. Acts 9. 34.
8. See II Corinthians 5. 16.
9. Romans 6. 23.
10. See section on Wholeness, p. 1f.
11. Genesis 1. 27, 31.
12. Ephesians 6. 12; cf. II Peter 2. 4.
13. *Against Heresies* IV, XX.

14. The New Missal.
15. See Chapter 3 on Evidence, p. 35 and Appendix Note A, p. 95.
16. Hebrews 6. 5.

2

Suffering

Faced with the vast amount of suffering on all hands today two questions immediately arise: 1) Why? 2) What can be done about it?

The Gospel of salvation throws much light upon the meaning and purpose of suffering. There is truth in the saying that what came into the world by sin must go out by suffering. Creation works according to laws, the violation of which inevitably leads to disorder, imbalance and disharmony. The law of cause and effect between sin and disorder can often be traced, for example the widespread neurosis following in the wake of the evil of war; at other times the connection may not be so obvious, the effect may not follow immediately or be recognized for what it is.

Although the free-will of man is to some extent conditioned by factors beyond his control, both deep in the past history of the human race and in his own environment, nevertheless he is not a robot and has a degree of responsibility for actions which will increase or diminish the suffering in the world. This very freedom, the misuse of which has led and is leading to tragic and disastrous consequences, is at the same time the distinguishing characteristic which, together with a degree of creativity superior to that of the lower orders, gives him the dignity and distinctiveness of being the crown of creation. No self-respecting individual would wish it to be otherwise, provided adequate guidance and direction were also available for determining the right choice. Such guidance comes through reason, revelation, experience and a moral consciousness; provisions in this direction call for obedience if life is to find its true fulfilment.[1] Man must love that which is highest when he sees it but, alas, he does not always love it more than himself.

In considering the subject of suffering in relation to healing it must be recognized at the outset that there is a great difference between disease and suffering. Disease, by definition, is a deviation from the normal nature of man; in the Gospels it is invariably recognized as an enemy. Long before the time of Christ it was acknowledged that diseases of body, mind and spirit were evils to be fought. Today, healing disciplines have an ever-increasing knowledge of ways and means of combating or preventing disease, and they are, consciously or unconsciously, cooperating with God for the overcoming of evil.

The fact of disorder is registered by pain and suffering. These are not interchangeable terms. Pain is a neutral agent serving to notify that something is wrong; suffering does more than this; it can serve as an instrument for much good, including healing, and constitutes a challenge, a challenge addressed to the corporate body of humanity, since an individual isolated in his suffering may not be able to overcome it without help.

The positive value of suffering can be further seen in: (1) Its contribution to growth; (2) Its educational value; (3) For refining; (4) In the context of Christian healing it can be a weapon in the hand of love for combat with evil, an instrument for the healing work of redemption and reparation.

Its contribution to growth

It is self-evident that normally efficiency does not drop into one's lap but has to be worked for, for example the hours of work put in to become a professional musician. In the sphere of personality the same is true: while the initial qualities that make for a strong character are God-given, it is only by man's cooperation that they live and thrive, for example patience. Much is said in the New Testament about this and the need for such exercise. Here adversity can be seen as an opportunity for growth: one of the words used by S. Paul to describe charity is 'long-suffering', and he says further: 'Suffering is part of your training'.[2] It is contingent upon development, and growing pains have a rightful and useful place. The muscular training of the athlete has its counterpart in the exercise that strengthens character.

Its educational value

'A burnt child dreads the fire.' It is by seeing the consequences of wrong action in events outside himself, and by experiencing them in his own life that man can discern the value or otherwise of standards of action.

For refining

The analogy of the refiner's fire has often been used in relation to suffering. In the Book of Maccabees, suffering of this kind is spoken of as 'a sign of great benevolence'.[3] S. Paul knew this by experience: the blindness after his conversion helped the former proud Pharisee to learn his dependence upon God; the thorn in the flesh helped him to realize the reliability of all-sufficient grace. How far the sufferer avails himself of this depends upon his response. He can be resentful, frustrated and embittered by it. Disease is an evil that can degrade, and must at all times be fought. Often the suffering is so intense that one individual left in isolation is overwhelmed, and to use it constructively he will need the help of others. Here is a challenge to Christian healing, that the effective healing power of love both human and divine may enable him to turn the suffering to good purpose, and thus, triumphing over it, to become through the experience a finer and stronger personality.

An instrument for the healing work of redemption and reparation

Anyone with the most elementary knowledge of Christianity must realize that Christian healing is not a way of escape from suffering. Only a little realism in considering the horrors of death by crucifixion is enough to show that to take up one's cross to follow Christ inevitably involves both suffering and sacrifice. The neophyte is sealed at baptism with this sign; thenceforth he is committed to take his share in the ever-present work of the world's Redeemer. But this is not the whole picture; the Gospel is not only news of Good Friday but also of Easter, i.e., triumph through suffering, and this is the message proclaimed through-out the pages of the New Testament. It was in the power of the resurrection[4] that suffering could be met, transcended and caught up into the healing of the world by the alchemy of the Cross. This triumphant, victorious life is not in evidence today as outstandingly as it was in the early days of the Church, but still there is abundant evidence of the Spirit's activity, and where this is recognized and related to the healing of the whole man a power is seen at work beyond the range of what is known to science.

Behind the triumphant approach to suffering seen in Christianity lies the power of love. Frequently, it is the innocent who suffer. An illustration of this can be seen in the parable of the Prodigal Son. The father probably suffered more than the boy; the latter suffered from physical need, the former for unrequited love. Subsequently, however, the impact of his love on the boy may have drawn forth the sorrow that was healing, the sorrow of true repentance.[5]

This brings us to the most important use of suffering, namely for the healing work of redemption and reparation. It is a fact that the greatest saints have often been the greatest sufferers. When sin and true love meet suffering inevitably follows. From the days of S. Stephen, the first Christian martyr, down to the present day, numerous examples bear witness to this; S. Francis of Assisi for instance, or to come closer to the context of healing, S. Bernadette of Lourdes or S. Thérèse of Lisieux. In the present century evidence can be found in connection with Nazi concentration camps, and prison conditions behind the Iron Curtain, where there are followers of Christ who have endured not only physical torture, but the far greater suffering of mind and spirit.

In the crucifixion, infinite love confronted the sin of man, and Christ's suffering continues throughout history until sin is no more. It is this that inspires those who are members of his Body to give themselves to his healing, redemptive work. This love is not only life-giving but self-giving, for self-sacrifice is essential to the activity of love. In the conflict with evil, with sin and its consequences in disease, disharmony, etc., love does not count the cost, nor does the Christian in union with Christ opt out of his solidarity with suffering mankind. He remains wholly human, inheriting the legacy of ills handed down through generations, but he is empowered not only to triumph over evil, but actually to take it and turn it to good (using it like a boomerang). Christ in his incarnate life did just that: his death was the means of the salvation of the world, and he still lives in members of his Body to bring life and power that transforms suffering into an instrument of healing for mankind.[6]

It is the wheat that is crushed and the grapes that are pressed that provide the bread and the wine of life. It is natural for man to show courage; he was made in God's image, and possesses a great potential for good. The Cardinal Virtues are not the monopoly of Christians,[7] but within the regenerate there is a new power: while truly human they are partakers of the divine nature, and as such are endowed with power by the indwelling Spirit of God for outstanding witness. The disciples who fled on Good Friday were changed after Pentecost.

For the Christian living in line with the purpose of creation, abiding in Christ and Christ in him, there is a wholeness of body, mind and spirit that is strong to resist the onslaught of disease. He rides the storms and tensions of life in a special way, buoyed up by the Christian hope in the power of the risen, contemporary Christ, and strengthened by the grace of the sacraments.

Whilst those whose love for God and man is intense inevitably share gladly in the suffering consequent upon the impact of love and sin, there is a false attitude which has been prominent at some periods of history, and which is not absent at the present day. Because so much good may result from suffering some have failed to recognize that it is not the suffering that heals, but the love that inspires, and the grace given to overcome suffering. This misunderstanding leads them either to seek suffering for its own sake or, when it comes, to adopt an attitude of resignation. Here it is important to recognize the difference between resignation and abandonment. Resignation can lead to inertia which is a serious obstacle to healing; abandonment to God does not rule out active cooperation with the means of healing. Indeed, such positive abandonment may prove the necessary condition for healing, giving the peace and poise that sets free the healing forces of nature and the healing grace of God.

There are sufferings which appear on the surface incompatible with belief in the love of God, for example the suffering of the innocent, although one may be able to recognize the solidarity of humanity and the benefits both to themselves and to others which this might serve.[8]

Then too there are natural disasters such as earthquakes, volcanic eruptions, typhoons, etc. Our limited visio.1 may not be able to see the reason for all this – no one has a right to expect to understand all the mysterious workings of God – but there are considerations that can help. God created, and he saw that it was good. At the same time, He would know the consequences of allowing a limited degree of creativity and free-will to man; but rather than deprive 'the crown of creation' of so great a dignity He made provision accordingly, some of the effects of which can be appreciated.

There is the boomerang use of suffering already mentioned. S. Gregory[9] said that Christ's answer to the doubts of S. Thomas was more useful to him than the certainty of the Magdalene who believed at once.

Christ's answer to S. Paul's thrice-repeated prayer for the removal of his 'thorn in the flesh', 'My strength is made perfect in [your] weakness', is often more help to those who feel this weakness than to those who have never experienced it. It must be noted, however, in passing that as regards this thorn in the flesh we are neither told what it was, nor whether it was eventually healed; all we know for certain is that S. Paul's magnificent evangelistic work continued until his eventual martyrdom.

The experience of grace given at times of suffering is well known; for example a certain sufferer whose neck was broken in a car accident, but who with modern skill was wonderfully healed, said that this misfortune had given her an entirely new outlook on life. To some, the same kind of experience has drawn them from agnosticism to faith, and for Christians has deepened the reality of their faith. This is not to be attributed to the misfortune in itself, which can bring bitterness and despair, but to the triumphant grace of God.

Another, and universal provision is the suffering caused by granting to man only a limited span of mortal life. But however much technology may prolong this, in relation to eternity its length is comparatively negligible, 'one night in a bad inn,' as S. Teresa called it.[10] God sent prophets to recall man to Himself, and last of all his Only-Begotten Son. 'God loved the world so much that He gave His only Son ... so that through Him the world might be saved'.[11] Moreover, He revealed the way of joy

through suffering and sacrifice, and brought life and immortality
to light.

> The troubles which are soon over, though they weigh little,
> train us for the carrying of a weight of eternal glory which is
> out of all proportion to them. And so we have no eyes for
> things that are visible, but only for the things that are invisible;
> for visible things last only for a time, and the invisible things
> are eternal.[12]

This is the Christian faith inspired by the resurrection which
reveals the truth that man was made for immortality, so that
through all time the Christian faced with death can, in the words
of R. L. Stevenson, say: 'Home is the sailor, home from sea, And
the hunter home from the hill'.[13] It is in this context that the
whole problem of suffering must be faced.

The sufferer in the midst of his suffering may not be able to appreciate the reasons for it, and much will depend upon his previous Christian training and experience, and upon those seeking
to help him. He has the compassion and strength of the ever-
present contemporary Christ, who by his own experience,
which included Gethsemane and Calvary, knows and under-
stands.

Christ plumbed the depths Himself, and knows how to make
suffering worthwhile, creative and of value instead of being a
waste. He supplies grace to meet need, and reveals to the individual the love and care of God: 'Every hair of your head has
been counted.'[14] The Christian with faith is able to say with
Mother Julian of Norwich: 'All shall be well, and all manner of
things shall be well.'[15]

This chapter has been concerned with the theological position.
How the practical application of this theory is to be viewed
remains for consideration. With this aim, the following chapter
will give some evidence from early history, and a later chapter
will deal with the present-day application of healing in relation
to both Christian and non-Christian in the ministry of the Body
of Christ.

Chapter notes

1. See Matthew 5. 17, 18.
2. Hebrews 12. 7.
3. 2 Maccabees 6. 13.
4. See Philippians 3. 10.
5. cf. the suffering of S. Monica before the conversion of S. Augustine.
6. See Romans 8. 37–39.
7. See for example the list of Old Testament heroes in Hebrews XI, the Maccabees, or the Greek heroes.
8. cf. The Holy Innocents.
9. *Homily 29 on the Gospels*.
10. *Way of Perfection*, Ch. 40.
11. John 3. 16, 17.
12. 2 Corinthians 4. 17, 18.
13. *Underwood XXI*.
14. Matthew 10. 30.
15. *Revelations of Divine Love*.

3

Evidence

In considering what the foregoing theology means for practical purposes the observer is confronted with one unique historical fact: 'The Word was made flesh and dwelt among us'. This inaugurated life in a new dimension with unprecedented consequences – consequences which exceed known natural laws.

The eye-witnesses faithfully record that Christ raised the dead, cleansed lepers, cast out devils, commanded the wind and waves and finally burst the bonds of death. The records do not end there. The advent of a Second Adam was the beginning of a new era. The Spirit of God Himself became incorporate in a body of believers, accompanied by powers similar to those manifested by Christ in the days of his flesh, and also by greater powers according to His promise:[1] for the believers were no longer merely friends and associates of His, but were themselves the Body of Christ, members of a new creation in which the divine was incarnate to a remarkable degree.

The history of the early Church reads like a commentary on Mark 16, 17–20; starting from the Acts of the Apostles and on through the years of persecution down to the time of the Emperor Constantine the evidence is clear that the Lord was working with them, and confirming the word by 'the signs that will be associated with believers'.[2]

When due allowance has been made for heightened records, credulity, etc., the nature, quality and cumulative amount of evidence is convincing. Many of the writers in whose work this evidence is to be found were scholars, for example the heads of the Catechetical School of Alexandria. Much of the writing was addressed to a critical, non-Christian world, to emperors and senators who knew how to weigh evidence and who were, in general, opposed to Christianity. Then there was the appeal of the Apologists for people to see with their own eyes the facts recorded. Onlookers were amazed at the attitude of Christians to torture and death. The raising of the dead, of which there are records in the New Testament, is also a well-known feature in the subsequent history.

There are three main directions in which the power of the risen and victorious contemporary Christ, working through his Spirit in the Church, can be seen, namely in the attitude to persecution, in power over the forces of evil and in healing the sick and raising the dead.

Evidence in relation to persecution

Christians triumphed amidst the severest tortures, acknowledging that their power came from union with Christ. Their witness had a marked effect upon onlookers and drew many to Christ. This was the case at a later date in our own country in the martyrdom of S. Alban. 'Dost thou not see them thrown to the wild beasts and yet not overcome? . . . these look not like the works of a man; they are the power of God; they are the proofs of his presence'.[3] There were instances of those thrown to wild beasts and emerging untouched.[4]

A graphic account of these persecutions is given in *On the Glory of Martyrdom*,[5] and in the *Passion of Perpetua and Felicitas*. In the *Passion* Perpetua replies to the servants' questions as to how she will face being thrown to the beasts: 'Then there will be Another in me, who will suffer for me because I am about to suffer for him.'[6]

The historian Eusebius preserves fragments of a letter from the Churches of Lyons and Vienne describing the persecution there and gives an account of the magnificent steadfastness of the martyrs, particularly of Sanctus, a deacon, Maturus, a late convert, Ponticus, a teenager, and the heroic Blandina: 'never among them has a woman endured so many and such terrible tortures'. Eusebius says 'everyone who suffers for the glory of Christ has fellowship always with the living God'.[7]

These are just some examples of the early witness to the faith; references and instances abound throughout the writings of the Ante-Nicene Church, and will repay study. A selection is given in Appendix Note A.

Such witness continues throughout the history of the church. It is quite possible that if all the facts of persecution in the twentieth century were known the evidence provided would be even greater than in any earlier century, though it must be remembered that the Church has increased in number from the 3,000 after Pentecost to the more than 985,000,000 of this century.[8]

Writing at the beginning of the fourth century S. Athanasius says: 'A very strong proof of the destruction of death and its conquest by the cross is supplied by a present fact, namely this: all the disciples of Christ despise death; they take the offensive against it and, instead of fearing it, by the sign of the cross and by faith in Christ trample on it as something dead'.[9]

Evidence in relation to power over the forces of evil

The work of exorcism has dominical authority. In the Gospels there are twelve accounts of exorcism by Christ himself before his Ascension, not including the six accounts of healing multitudes, amongst whom were probably similar cases. Healings of this description were recorded in the missions both of the Twelve and the Seventy; in the latter case Christ's reply to the report of such healings was: 'Yes I have given you power to tread underfoot ... the whole strength of the enemy.'[10] Before the Ascension, in final instructions to the Apostles he said: 'These are the signs that will be associated with believers ... in my name they will cast out devils.'[11] S. Paul mentions amongst the gifts of the Spirit that of 'recognizing spirits'.[12]

The fact that much which in the first century was attributed to demons can now be classified under terminology found in textbooks of modern science may change the labels but cannot alter the fact of the cures; in some instances there is ground for thinking that if such cases were treated in twentieth-century mental hospitals they would not come out healed.

The quantity and quality of evidence of these healings is such that it would be presumptuous to deny the diagnosis in all cases, but however few or many, it is not the number of healings in this respect that provides the strongest evidence, but the principle behind them. The Church of the New Testament was so convinced that all authority was given to Christ in heaven and on earth that there was no room for the pagan dualism found in the world around them. They were keenly conscious that 'it is not against human enemies that we have to struggle, but against the Sovereignties and Powers who originate the darkness in this world, the spiritual army of evil in the heavens'.[13] They knew that there was only one true God and that the Prince of the Powers of Darkness was under His command. Thus they fearlessly used His delegated authority to bind, rebuke, and subjugate forces of evil wherever found.

These healings, so numerous in the early days and which in many cases showed clear signs of possession, rested upon this one fundamental principle: namely, the supreme authority of God in all circumstances. This principle never failed when applied by Christ, nor in the early years after Pentecost; in a sense the classification of results mattered little, all were healed. Even as late as the third century Origen could write: 'The Name of Jesus can still remove distractions from the minds of men, and expel demons, and also take away diseases'.[14]

Considerable reference to such healings is found in the writings of the Ante-Nicene Church, and Justin Martyr suggests that a Jew using the name of the God of Abraham, Isaac and Jacob might equally effectively exorcise,[15] whilst those who tried to imitate the Christian from unworthy motives were unsuccessful;[16] the Christians were able to heal where the pagans could not do so.[17]

It is important, however, to recognize that there is nothing magical or automatic about this. Before Pentecost, in the days when the disciples were being trained by Christ there is one instance when they failed in what in those days was regarded as a case of possession, but which more probably was a case of epilepsy. The answer Christ gave to their question as to why they failed gives a clear indication of the technique of these early healings, namely that they were not the result of any human skill or insight, they were spiritual ministrations; the requisite was prayer and probably, as in other instances, fasting. The failure of the disciples on this particular occasion[18] was caused by the unspiritual nature of their behaviour at the time. From what follows,[19] it seems they were disputing about who was the greatest, no doubt as a result of the selection of three to ascend the mount with Jesus. This cause of inability to heal in later centuries was noted both in relation to physical healing and to exorcism.

Lactantius, for example, writing early in the fourth century prefaces his account of exorcisms by the words: 'as long as there is peace among the people of God';[20] and this is put very definitely in relation to physical healing by S. Cyprian in the middle of the third century.[21]

Thus it is not surprising that as the first fervour of the primitive Church lessened, particularly after the conversion of Constantine and the subsequent unification of the Church, regulations relating to exorcism became necessary.

Evidence in healing the sick and raising the dead

The writer of the appendix to the fourth Gospel says that if all Christ's works were written down 'the world itself, I suppose, would not hold all the books that would have to be written'.[22] The reference here is to the work of Christ in the days of his flesh, but this was just the beginning; although Christ's presence was in a different dimension after the Resurrection his work never ceased. The Resurrection guaranteed for the early Church his continued presence, unchanging power and the continuity of the work which S. Luke traces in the Acts of the Apostles, which continues to the present day and, according to his promise, will do so 'to the end of time'.[23]

Of the forty-one records of cures in the Gospels, thirty-three to thirty-seven refer to physical cures; of the nineteen in the Acts thirteen to nineteen do so. Passing beyond the pages of the New Testament the records are so numerous that writers frequently use words such as 'daily' in narrating them.

Several of these writers explain these cures on the grounds that all life comes from God, that Christ is God and the Church in Christ is therefore in direct contact with the source of all life; since God is pre-eminently supreme in knowledge and power, things impossible to men are possible to Him, and thus can be mediated to men through his Body the Church.[24] Like S. Paul, Christians can speak of the things Christ has wrought through them.[25] To mediate his healing in this way was a recognized duty, so much so that to fail was regarded as a great sin.[26]

It was claimed that Christ still healed, as in the days of his flesh, all who believed in him and called upon his name. The list of diseases healed cover all kinds, both organic and functional, and there were frequent instances of raising the dead, which S. Irenaeus says: 'has been frequently done in the brotherhood on account of some necessity – the entire Church in that particular locality entreating the boon with much fasting and prayer'.[27] Other writers of this period give similar testimony. Such healings, including the raising of the dead, did not cease with the close of these early years, but the first fervour began to give place to controversy, and there was need of a compass for those whose task it was to steer the ship of the Church through the troubled waters of heresy – and such a compass was supplied by the Creeds.

S. Cyprian in the middle of the third century wrote:

> Eager about our patrimony and our gain, seeking to satisfy our pride, yielding ourselves wholly to emulation and strife, careless of simplicity and faith, renouncing the world in words only, and not in deeds, every one of us pleasing himself, and displeasing all others ... while we despise the commandments of the Lord ... the enemy was receiving a power of doing mischief, and was overwhelming, by the cast of his net, those who were imperfecty armed, and too careless to resist.[28]

When S. Paul corrected something of this kind in the Corinthian Church he pointed out its association with ill health. At the end of the fourth century the sermons of S. John Chrysostom show to what a serious extent these abuses had grown.

There is no need to look further to see why more healing is not found in later periods of Church history; its presence is a notable feature at times of revival and in the lives of the saints, and the wonder is rather that evidence for so much has persisted down the centuries, and still continues at the present day.[29]

Chapter notes

1. John 14. 12.
2. Mark 16. 20.
3. *Epistle to Diognetus*, Ch. 7.
4. See for example Ignatius, *Epistle to Romans*, Ch. 5.
5. Pseudo Cyprian, Ch. 6.
6. *Passion of Perpetua and Felicitas*, Chs. 3 and 4.
7. *History* VI.

8. These are the 1971 statistics.
9. *De Incarnatione*, V. 27.
10. Luke 10. 19.
11. Mark 16. 17–20.
12. I Corinthians 12. 10.
13. Ephesians 6. 12.
14. *Against Celsus*, I. 67.
15. *Dialogue with Trypho*, Ch. 85.
16. See Acts 19. 13.
17. Justin Martyr, *Apology to the Senate*, II. 6.
18. Mark 9. 17–29.
19. Mark 9. 34.
20. *The Divine Institutes*, II. 6.
21. See p. 40.
22. John 21. 25.
23. Matthew 28. 20.
24. Irenaeus, *Against Heresies*, II. 10. 4.
25. Acts 15. 12.
26. *Shepherd of Hermas*, Sim: 10. 4.
27. *Against Heresies*, II. 31. 2.
28. *Epistle 6*, 1–4.
29. Appendix Note A, p. 95 gives a selection of evidence taken from the writings of the Ante-Nicene Church.

4

Means of healing in the Early Church

The Eucharist

The Bread of the Sacrament is a food for the body and a strong medicine even for corporal ills.[1]

The Church is a healing body, and wherever one studies closely the liturgy whether eastern or western one finds, however much the emphasis may shift, that it is full of healing for body as well as for soul. This can be found in words of administration, collects and elsewhere. The wording in the Anglican Books of Common Prayer of 1548 and 1549 is well known, for example in the Prayer of Humble Access: 'That our sinful bodies may be made clean by His Body, and our souls washed through His most precious Blood'. In the previous Roman Missal the word 'body' disappeared from the form of administration; in the new Missal the words have returned to those used in the fourth or even the third century.

The priest's prayer immediately preceding the Communion was that it may be 'a safeguard and a healing remedy both of soul and body', and in the new rite, 'Let It not bring me condemnation, but health in mind and body'. In the collect of the mass for the sick are the words: 'We humbly crave the help of thy mercy, that, being restored to health, they may render thanks to thee in thy Church'. In the Eastern Liturgy, in the thanksgiving after Communion are the words: 'Benefactor of our souls and bodies'[2] and 'Thy holy ... Mysteries, which Thou has given us for the welfare and sanctification and healing of souls and bodies'.[3]

In the Eastern Church communion has always been in both kinds, through intinction, as it was in the West until the twelfth century. Among theologians of the Middle Ages the idea was fairly common that the Body was for our bodies and the Blood for our souls.

From the earliest times this highest means of healing was taken to sick members. Dom Gregory Dix, commenting on the changes that have taken place in the liturgy says: 'The old eschatological understanding of the Eucharist as the irruption into time of the heavenly Christ and of the Eucharist as actualizing an eternal redemption in the present earthly Church as the Body of Christ even in this world, was replaced by a new insistence on the purely historical achievement of redemption within the world by Christ at a particular moment and by particular actions in the past'.[4]

This change in the climate of thought had repercussions on the doctrine and practice of divine healing. The twentieth century has seen a re-focusing of attention upon the Primitive Church, and this return to a fuller appreciation of her mind and spirit has direct bearing on the healing ministry of the Church: it is no mere coincidence that it comes at the same time as movements towards a fuller restoration of this ministry.

The use of oil

The Twelve 'cast out many devils and anointed many sick people with oil and cured them'.[5]

This is probably the earliest experience the disciples themselves had of practising the anointing of the sick. They were sent out with power and authority for this by Christ. When the Seventy were also sent out and instructed to heal, anointing is not specifically mentioned; but it is undoubtedly from this early training of the disciples that the practice was recognized as having dominical authority.

To use oil in healing was no new custom; it was used both by Jew and Gentile in religious rites and as a medicinal remedy. Those anointed by the disciples and their successors would be familiar with the association of oil with healing. It was, therefore, a fitting instrument by means of which the power and authority of Christ could find a focus in the healing work of the Church. It is not surprising that from apostolic times down to the present day this has been one of the ways by which the contemporary Christ brings his healing power and authority to bear in the conquest of disease. In the Epistle of S. James it is expressly recommended:

> If one of you is ill, he should send for the elders of the church, and they must anoint him with oil in the name of the Lord and pray over him. The prayer of faith will save the sick man and the Lord will raise him up again.[6]

As early as the third century there is to be found in Church Orders provision for the blessing of oil for anointing the sick, and at an even earlier date oil was being blessed for pre-baptismal exorcisms. These blessings took place at the Eucharist.

Two examples of early forms of this blessing during the Eucharist are:

> O Lord God, who has given us the Paraclete Spirit, the Lord, the saving name, the immutable Spirit, who is hidden from the foolish, but revealed to the wise: Christ who hast sanctified us, who by thy mercy hast made thy servants wise, those whom thou hast chosen in thy wisdom; who hast sent us sinners the knowledge of thy Spirit, through thy holiness, when thou didst grant us the virtue of thy Spirit; who cureth all sickness and all suffering; thou who hast given the gift of healing to all who have become worthy of such a gift, send down upon this oil, the image of thy fecundity, the fullness of thy merciful goodness, that it may deliver those who are in pain, that it may cure those who are sick, that it may sanctify those who return (those who are converted) when they come to the faith, for thou art strong and glorious for everlasting ages.

This is probably the earliest known form, taken from a Syrian document, *The Testament of our Lord Jesus Christ*. The precise date of this is unknown, but it is probably pre-Nicene, and may even go back to the second century. Both the sick and the baptismal candidate are envisaged here, whereas in the West at the present time there are three separate blessings, all very ancient, of oil, (a) for the catechumen, (b) for the sick and (c) for use at baptism, and can be dated prior to the sixth century.

We bless through the name of thy only-begotten Jesus Christ these creatures; we name the name of Him who suffered, who was crucified and rose again, and who sitteth on the right hand of the uncreated, upon this water and upon this oil. Grant healing power upon these creatures, that every fever and every evil spirit and every sickness may depart through the drinking and the anointing; and that the partaking of these creatures may be a healing medicine, and a medicine of soundness, in the name of thy only-begotten son Jesus Christ, through whom to thee is the glory and the strength in the Holy Spirit through all the ages of the ages'[7]

This is from a Greek manuscript, discovered on Mount Athos, in the Pontifical of S. Serapion, Bishop of Thumis, *c.* AD 339. The custom there was for the faithful to bring oil, water and bread to be blessed at the Eucharist and taken away for use. [8]

The Laying on of Hands by those duly authorized

These are the signs that will be associated with believers; in my name they will cast out devils ... they will lay hands on the sick, who will recover.[9]

The Laying on of Hands was a recognized form of blessing in the Old Testament and naturally passed into use in the Christian Church. It was frequently used by Christ,[10] and the Apostles would adopt the same methods used by their Master. S. Paul used it for the healing of the father of Publius in Malta.[11] There were those who possessed some special gift of healing in this way, but it is important to remember that it was not the individual but the activity of Christ operating through him which helped the sufferer by using the Laying on of Hands as an outward sign and focus.

In the early Church this became the first customary way of healing the sick by those ministering a charisma of healing, and also in the regular rite for the Visitation of the Sick. The use of oil, however, came to be more associated with healing the sick when the ministry was to the faithful, whilst the Laying on of Hands became more used in connection with exorcism, but this was by no means an invariable custom. Later, when anointing became usual in the rite for the Visitation of the Sick, some of the prayers retained, and still retain, reference to the Laying on of Hands; in some rites both are found. A Milanese rite of anointing is actually called *Manus impositio*.

A variant of this practice was the laying of the Book of the Gospels on the head of the sufferer in token of his faith in the truth of Christ's teaching and in his power to heal. This rite can be found as early as the fourth century, and included psalms, prayers and passages from the Gospels. This rite, with modifications, has been retained in both East and West. In the current Western Rite 'of the Care of the Sick', the priest lays his right hand on the sufferer's head, repeating the words of the Gospel: 'They shall lay their hands on the sick and they shall recover'. The rite retains some very ancient prayers. In the East, at the end of the rite of Holy Unction the ancient rite of placing the Book on the sufferer's head is still retained.

The use of the name

> In my name they shall cast out devils ... they shall lay their hands on the sick and they shall recover.[12]

As has previously been stated, a person's name could be far more than an 'identification label'; something of the power of the personality was inherent in the name. Just as the Jews, who would not use the sacred name in common speech, used it for exorcism and healing, so the Christians used the name of Jesus. This has been a frequent means of healing throughout the history of the Church, both East and West. To invoke his name was to bring the power and authority of his personal presence to bear upon the situation.

In the New Testament the Seventy sent out by Christ returned and reported: 'Lord, even the devils submit to us when we use your name'.[13] S. Peter used it in the healing of the lame cripple, and subsequently explained to the people the cause of this healing.[14] At Philippi S. Paul used it for healing the soothsayer.[15] One fourth century example of its use can be seen in the Pontifical of S. Serapion.[16] Writing in the same century, Arnobius said that the invocation of the Name puts to flight evil spirits, imposes silence on seers, leaves augurs unanswered, is able to render ineffective the operations of boastful magicians, not through the terror inspired ... but by the exercise of a greater authority.[17]

This use of the Name both for exorcism and all manner of healing is frequent throughout the history of the Church, both East and West. In the West notable exponents of its power include S. Bernard (1090–1153), S. Bernardino of Siena (1380–1444) and S. Giovanni Capistrano (1386–1456).

> The name of Jesus is ... a sovereign medicine. ... In dangers and distress, in fears and anxieties, let him call on this name of power and his confidence will return, his peace of mind will be restored. ... There is no ill of life, no adversity of misfortune, in which this adorable name will not bring help and fortitude.[18]

Anyone who knows anything of the Eastern Church will know how great is the importance placed there on the use of the Name. Years of experience cannot exhaust the possibility of healing and blessing that are found in the use of the Jesus Prayer.

> Only our lack of bold faith and charity prevents us from calling upon the Name in the power of the Spirit. ... He whose heart is become a vessel of the Holy Name should not hesitate to go about and repeat to those who need spiritual or bodily relief the words of Peter, 'Silver and gold have I none but such as I have I give thee in the Name of Jesus'.[19]

This use of the name is very far removed from name magic. To use it for one's own purpose is magic, to commit trustfully to Christ's purpose is faith. 'The name is nothing without the presence. ... The presence of Jesus is the real content and substance of the Holy Name. The Name both signifies Jesus' presence and brings its reality'.[20] This statement provides a clue to this means of healing and a deterrent to its abuse. The fate of the seven sons of Sceva[21] is not an isolated instance of misuse; it has often been used in a magical, mechanical and egotistic way which does more harm than good. This should be a warning but not an argument against its proper use; it shows the need for a clear understanding and teaching about how to use in the right way this very powerful means of healing.

Exorcism

Christ was able with authority to command, rebuke, direct. The resurrection confirmed his complete and decisive victory over evil. Pentecost meant that the power of this victory resided within his body on earth by his indwelling spirit.

In the early centuries all disease was regarded as having a diabolic origin, and exorcism was a frequent practice in healing work. The close association between disease and a personal agency of evil led to its practice in cases which would be diagnosed and treated differently today.

The means used were very varied. They included the use of the Name, of the Sign of the Cross, of holy water and insufflation (i.e. breathing upon the one being exorcized), Laying on of Hands, the narration of stories of the life of Christ, giving something to eat such as blessed bread or water, and a command or rebuke to the evil spirit in the name of Christ.

In the early days after Pentecost no long preparation for baptism was necessary. The Ethiopian, Cornelius and the gaoler at Philippi appear to have been baptized as soon as they confessed their belief in Christ; but as Christianity spread and particularly because of persecution, a more thorough preparation was recognized as necessary. Before the convert from paganism could become a full member of the Body of Christ a total severance from his former paganism was required, and thus in the course of his catechumenate he was frequently exorcized, and at his baptism after he had made his act of renunciation of Satan a solemn exorcism with anointing was performed by the bishop. Thus there grew up an order of exorcists whose special function was these pre-baptismal exorcisms. The history of this order shows a gradual marked development in correspondence with the conditions of the time. In some quarters these exorcists were drawn from the ranks of the monks, and in the early days their office was only temporary, though the evidence available shows a very varied length of tenure. They were appointed or commissioned by the bishop. The term 'ordained' only came into use later, when ordination to the order came to be regarded as a first

step towards ordination to higher orders. They were not ordained by the Laying on of Hands, but were ranked among the
eight minor orders which included acolytes, doorkeepers,
readers, etc. The first evidence of a special 'Ordering' of these
exorcists dates from the time of the Council of Carthage in AD
256. They were very numerous in the late third and the fourth
centuries; one, Peter, martyred under the Emperor Diocletian, is
mentioned in the Canon of the Roman Mass.

At his 'Ordering' the candidate was handed a book of exorcisms and told to learn them by heart, he was commissioned by
the bishop for the Laying on of Hands and for exorcism of candi-
dates for baptism. In the beginning it appears that his authority
was strictly limited to these, but by the time Isidore of Seville
(560–636) writes of them it is clear that their authority had
become much wider, and included the baptized as well as the
catechumens. The words of their ordering were: 'Take this book
and commit it to memory, and receive power to lay hands on
energumens[22] be they baptized or be they catechumens.'

This shows that by this time only those authorized by the
bishop were allowed such functions; the regulation to this effect
was made about AD 372.[23] Until then there were those outside
the Order who practised it, but this was open to abuse and no
doubt provided good reason for regularization. In the middle of
the third century S. Cyprian tells of a certain appointed exorcist:

> a man approved and always of good conversation in respect of
> religious discipline; who, stimulated by the exhortation also of
> very many brethren who were themselves strong and praise-
> worthy in the faith, raised himself up against that wicked
> spirit to overcome it . . . That exorcist, inspired by God's
> grace, bravely resisted.[24]

It is noteworthy that none of the 'very many brethren' in spite of
their strong faith attempted to exorcize the woman, nor did any
of the priests, but they appealed to the exorcist.

After the days when the catechumenate played so prominent a
part, i.e. from the sixth century, the Order of Exorcists fell more
into the background. Two are mentioned in the sixth century,
but admission to the Order was by now regarded as a first stage
to higher orders, and was still so regarded until a few years ago,
though the wording of the rite was almost the same as that used

in the sixth century; the main difference was that instead of the candidate being handed a book of exorcisms, he was handed a missal or pontifical.[25]

The sacerdotal blessing

There was need not only for exorcism before baptism but also for protection afterwards. The child of God could be given the assurance of the protective enfoldment within a Body vital with the love and power of God; there was therefore, in theory, no longer a need for casting out evil from within, but only for protection from evil without. In addition to the grace of sacrament and prayer, details of his daily life could be hallowed by a special blessing to encourage and remind him of his participation in the Kingdom of Light, with its power to overcome all onslaughts of the powers of darkness, whether on body, mind or spirit.

Part of the priest's ordination endowment was special power over these forces of evil, 'that whatever they bless may be blessed, and whatever they consecrate may be consecrated'. This sacerdotal blessing was an outward sign of something spiritually powerful; in a sense it could be regarded as complementary to exorcism. It could be given not only to persons but to inanimate objects, for example, houses. When such blessings are formally given two factors are always included: the Sign of the Cross and the use of Holy Water – thus giving greater spiritual force to the benediction.

Holy Water

Evidence of water that had been specially consecrated being used for healing purposes goes back to the second century. The Edict of Gratian (Emperor of Rome AD 375–85) ruled that this water was to be exorcized, blessed by the priest and sprinkled with exorcized salt. Thus there grew up a ritual found in the early Sacramentaries of the Church which is still used by the Church, both Eastern and Western. In the blessing prayers it is expressly stated that the water should be used for healing of soul and body and 'that whatsoever is touched or sprinkled with it may be freed from all uncleanness and from all assaults of the evil spirit'. After the Sign of the Cross is made over the water the final prayer asks: 'Wherever it shall be sprinkled and thy holy Name shall be invoked in prayer, every assault of the unclean spirit may be baffled ... and the presence of the Holy Spirit everywhere vouchsafed.'

These venerable and widespread customs have since the Reformation largely fallen into disuse in many quarters, owing to some extent to the way in which, without careful teaching upon their spiritual meaning and content, they can and frequently have degenerated into superstition or merely mechanical use. But this abuse of such long-standing and universal rites does not invalidate the customs themselves which, when used carefully and prayerfully as the sacramentals they are meant to be, can still prove of great benefit – even though the forces of evil against which Christian warfare is waged are now, in this scientific age, rightly or wrongly, thought of in a more impersonal way than in the ages when these rites originated.

The prayer of faith – corporate or individual

Because man is not pure spirit he normally needs the help of outward and visible signs as a means of contact with the spiritual, but he is not essentially dependent upon such, and there are those whose vital contact with God is by pure faith.

There are many definitions of faith. The catechism of the Council of Trent says:

> Faith so sharpens the power of the human intelligence that it can penetrate heaven without effort and, flooded with the light of God, it becomes able to reach first of all the Fount of Light, thence proceeds to all things below God ... in such a way that we experience with great exultation the truth that we are called out of darkness into His admirable light.[26]

S. John of the Cross states: 'Faith gives and communicates to us God Himself'.[27]

The New Testament speaks of it thus: 'Only faith can guarantee the blessings that we hope for, or prove the existence of the realities that at present remain unseen.'[28] Let us not lose sight of Jesus, who leads us in our faith and brings it to perfection'.[29] Calling Christians to imitate the heroes of faith of old, the New

Testament speaks of the Christian hope as 'an anchor for our soul, as sure as it is firm, and reaching right through beyond the veil'.[30]

Christian faith is essentially personal, the hope to which it gives substance being the end for which man is created, namely God, revealed and made accessible in Christ. It is a faith that becomes the eye of the soul that sees Him, and the anchor of the soul that holds Him fast.

The faith in Christ recorded in the Gospels bears this out. The impression left on onlookers who witnessed his healing work was 'God hath visited his people'.[31] The insight given to the disciples was: 'You are the Christ, the Son of the living God.'[32]

Faith such as this is the key to healing through the prayer of faith. The classic example of it in the Gospels is the healing of the centurion's servant, a faith highly commended by Christ.[33] Another instance is the Syrophoenician mother's prayer for her daughter.[34] This faith even 'if no bigger that a mustard seed can move mountains and nothing will prove impossible'.[35] To it is attached the promise: 'If you ask for anything in My Name, I will do it'.[36]

This direct approach in faith, whether corporate or individual, is to be seen all through the history of the Church. One has only to recall the lives of such saints as S. Bernard, S. Vincent Ferrer or S. Francis Xavier, to mention only three, in whose lives the healing ministry was conspicuous, particularly at times of revival.

The Liturgy as it developed through the centuries is full of prayers for healing of both body and soul. Intercession by name at church or in groups, present either bodily or in spirit, can be a strong means of healing through the prayer of faith. The Christian belief in the unity of the members of the Body of Christ and the consequent communion of saints means that the faithful in the Church Triumphant were called upon as joint intercessors, especially such saints as were outstanding in their powerful intercession while still on earth. This can be seen from the days of the catacombs onwards, sometimes in association with the use of sacred images, relics, pilgrimages to sacred shrines such as Lourdes, or – in our own country – Walsingham; in the East it can be found in association with icons, many of which were reputed to be miraculous.

Religion and medicine

Religion and medicine are both directed towards healing, and recognize that disease, as a derangement of the natural order, is an evil to be combated. It is not surprising therefore that from the earliest days Christianity has been in the forefront of those using such medical skill as the insight of the day provided.

From the time when S. Luke accompanied S. Paul on his evangelistic work – and it should be noted that it was the 'Beloved Physician' who recorded the healing work performed through his evangelistic companion, not vice versa – there have been doctors in the Church who have used such medical knowledge as was available.

Probably the best-known doctors of the Early Church are the two brothers from Arabia, SS. Cosmos and Damian, who gave their services free, and were much loved and sought after because of the widespread fame of their cures. Even to the present day they are venerated, regarded as the patron saints of doctors, and appealed to for help especially in the Eastern Church, together with another doctor of about the same period – *c*. AD 305 who also treated patients free, namely S. Panteleon, and who according to tradition was physician to the Emperor Galarius at Nicomedia.

The Gospels leave no doubt as regards God's will concerning the care and cure of the sick, and there were always individuals who recognized that practical Christianity demanded such care for the poor, the needy and the sick; thus quite naturally institutions for help and treatment sprang up. There are records of the early stages of pioneering efforts where Christian help was organized for the sick. During a famine in Mesopotamia, S. Ephraim the Syrian (306–73) organized 300 ambulances for relief work; in the same century S. Basil established an institution for the help and treatment of lepers; S. Fabiola, probably helped by S. Pammachius, founded the first centre for the sick in Rome; others were established by S. Chrysostom and S. Augustine. By the fifth century there was an order of clerics known as the Parabolani, under episcopal supervision, devoted to nursing the sick; there are references to these in 416 and 418. This order originated in Alexandria, probably during some epidemic; later it was also working in Constantinople; membership was at first limited to 500, later to 600.

S. Benedict in his *Rule* aptly expresses the mind of the Church on this subject:

> Before all things and above all things care must be taken of the sick, so that they may be served in very deed as Christ himself; for he has said 'I was sick and ye visited me' and 'what ye did to one of these least ones ye did unto me.'[37]

Thus the Church, not only through its sacramental, charismatic and other means of healing already mentioned, but in the building of hospitals, the founding of nursing orders, the service of the sick in times of plague or famine and in many other ways has done outstanding, often pioneer work. In succeeding centuries this was to expand widely, especially through the monastic orders.[38]

The knowledge and skill of doctors, the analytical gifts of the scientist, the tenderness and patience of nurses, the compassion of those who would now be termed social workers were all recognized as gifts by means of which the healing power of God is mediated to mankind.

The fact that a process of healing can be traced to the working of a natural law does not eliminate the possibility of an immanent divine activity. The unexpected beneficial change of environment or other circumstances of the patient; the sudden light on a diagnosis; the coincidence of the best consultant being unexpectedly available – these may well have happened because someone, doctor, nurse, patient or friends, had been praying. The old Christian custom of writing the Sign of the Cross on the prescription need not be a mere formality; a Christian doctor can make this an act of committing the patient into the hands of God, and a prayer that God will use him to bring healing to the patient.

Chapter notes

1. S. Teresa of Avila.
2. Liturgy of S. John Chrysostom.
3. Liturgy of S. Basil.
4. *Shape of the Liturgy*, pp. 137 ff.
5. Mark 6. 13.
6. James 5. 14, 15.

7. The translation of these two forms of blessing is taken from F. Cabrol: *Liturgical Prayer, Its History and Spirit.*

8. For the subsequent history of Anointing and Extreme Unction see pp. 60, 78, 98.

9. Mark 16. 17, 18.

10. See Mark 6. 5; 5. 23; 7. 32; 8. 25.

11. Acts 28. 8.

12. Mark 16, 17, 18.

13. Luke 10. 17.

14. Acts 3. 6, 16; 4. 10.

15. Acts 16. 18.

16. Cited on p. 45.

17. *Adversus Gentes*, I, 46.

18. Sermons of S. Bernard on Advent and Christmas. Sermon 6 *On the Holy Name of Jesus.*

19. *On the Invocation of the Name of Jesus,* by a monk of the Eastern Church.

20. Ibid.

21. Acts 19. 4.

22. i.e. demoniacs.

23. See the *Canons of Laodicea.*

24. *Epistle* 74. 10.

25. See further, p. 80f.

26. *Catechism* Part Ic, II Q 6.

27. *Spiritual Canticle* 1, vol. II, p. 198.

28. Hebrews 11. 1.

29. Ibid. 12. 2.

30. Ibid. 6. 19.

31. Luke 7. 16.

32. Matthew 16. 16.

33. Luke 7. 1–10.

34. Mark 7. 25–30.

35. Matthew 17. 20.

36. John 14. 12–14.

37. *Rule*, Ch. 36.

38. For further details, see pp. 70–1.

5

The intervening years

The Middle Ages (fourth to fifteenth century)

The rapid expansion of the Church once Christianity became the accepted religion in the Roman Empire called for a more ordered and structured life than had been needed, or even possible, in the days of persecution.

Already the scriptures, so far as they had survived, were recognized as authoritative: guidelines for the interpretation of Christian experience were provided by the earlier creeds; these were essential in the stormy days of controversy when heresy created an imbalance that over-emphasized or denied one or other fundamental truth.

During the following centuries there was still considerable evidence of healing: there were those within the Body called to manifest a charisma of healing and exorcism, and other means of healing were in frequent demand.[1]

The minor order of exorcists was well established and prominent, but by the end of the third century it was regarded as the lowest office in the Church. When S. Hilary wished to ordain S. Martin of Tours[2] the latter refused but consented to become an exorcist, an office which he could not refuse lest he should seem to despise it on the grounds of its unimportance.

The lives of the saints at this period give plenty of examples of healing work,[3] and S. Cyril of Jerusalem[4] speaks of exorcism as a common practice in the fourth century. In the sixth century S. Gregory the Great[5] gives an insight into the Benedictine works of healing, both in his account of S. Benedict himself[6] and in his letter to S. Augustine of Canterbury[7] with its warning of the danger of vainglory from the very numerous miracles of healing resulting from the latter's ministry in England. S. Bede the Venerable[8] tells of miracles of healing through the prayers of the saints including those of S. Germanus,[9] S. Oswald[10] and S. Cuthbert.[11] Of other parts of Christendom the same can be said.

However much legend may be interwoven with records as we now have them, the fact remains that the existence of such miracles was a matter of common belief in those days. At the same time there is less evidence than during the exuberant life of the Primitive Church, and this decrease becomes more marked in later centuries; so much so that it was frequently said that the days of miracles of healing were over – although at no period of history were they absent, and indeed in the East this ministry proceeds in unbroken continuity.

Already a decrease in the practice of the Laying on of Hands can be noticed, except within rites for the visitation of the sick. Two reasons for this became traditional:

1. That the Laying on of Hands was meant more for witness to the pagan world: 'confirming the Word with signs following'; and so, with the spread of Christianity throughout the Roman Empire, the need for it became less.
2. That the charismatic gifts were only for the early days of the Church and had since been withdrawn – a theory which could not be borne out by subsequent history except, perhaps, in the modified form given by S. Gregory the Great, namely that God may sometimes temporarily withhold these gifts so that humility may be strengthened. Even so, S. Gregory does not – and in view of his own first-hand knowledge could not – say that they were at any time totally suppressed, only that there might be a decrease compared with primitive times.

It is more probable that the explanation given in the middle of the third century by S. Cyprian is more radically true – that the decrease in the power of healing was indicative of a lowering of spiritual vitality within the Church.[12]

The theology remained the same, namely that the power of the risen Christ to heal circulated through all members of his Body; but in practice the ministry came more into the hands of the clergy, although in these early centuries the laity were not debarred from using exorcism and other forms of ministry when they felt called upon to do so. Especially is this the case in the East.

Some interesting light is thrown upon the position at the beginning of the fifth century by a correspondence between Decentius, Bishop of Eugubium, and Pope Innocent I[13] in which the latter ruled that:

1. Those who after baptism became possessed were not to be exorcized until the bishop had given permission, and the exorcism was to be performed by one of the clergy specially delegated in each case to do this, using the Sign of the Cross and the Laying on of Hands.

2. Anointing might be performed by clergy or laity but only to the faithful communicants; those undergoing penance and thus debarred from the Eucharist might not be anointed, 'For it is a kind of sacrament. How can it be thought possible for one kind to be conferred on those to whom the rest of the sacraments are denied?'

More and more it came to be recognized that it was by the Church as the Body of Christ through the successors of the Apostles that healing was to be brought. Consecrated bread from the bishop's Mass had first to be taken to the sick; the bishop himself would minister to them when his duties allowed time. As early as the fourth century there was a rite for the Visitation of the Sick by the rural bishop[14] which appears to include anointing, although not until the twelfth century[15] is there reference to anointing as a formal sacrament. It was not yet a regular feature of the Visitation of the Sick but was on its way to becoming so.

There seems to have been an increase in the use of Holy Oil from the fifth century. The blessing of oil at the Eucharist for anointing the sick probably developed from the blessing of it at that time for the pre-baptismal exorcisms.[16] Sometimes the faithful brought their own oil. It was not unknown for them to take oil from the church lamps for this purpose.[17] They could then anoint themselves or their sick friends; husbands would take it for their wives if they needed it and women sometimes anointed the sick.[18] Reference to this custom can be found even as late as the eighth century.[19]

This somewhat free and easy use of Holy Oil called for teaching and regulation, more especially because Christians lived in a world where pagan practices, superstition and magic could and did lead to confusion of thought.

The pagans closely associated oil with healing, a view which went back 600 years or more BC to the magic, sorcery, hypnotism and so on practised by Greek priests on the sick. In the fifth century BC Hippocrates tried to dissociate medicine from priestcraft but popular thought would still easily revert to those ingrained, inherited ideas when confronted with an approach to healing through the Church. Much was done by church leaders to deal with this need;[20] authoritative steps were being taken by teaching and regulation to meet it.

Teaching

This was provided for by:

1. Reserving the blessing of the oil to once a year on Holy Thursday, when the bishop would at the same time give an explanation of his action.

    From the eighth century this was the general practice in the West but there were still, during the next 300 years, isolated instances of blessing by priests. In the East this practice was not adopted and the priest, not the bishop, would bless the oil; the parish priest still does so.
2. Reminding the faithful that the Holy Oil was not a magic talisman possessing automatic healing virtue, but an outward and visible sign of God's mercy conveyed through the power of the Holy Spirit and a means of receiving his healing in response to the prayer of faith accompanying the use of it.

Regulation

This was provided for by encouraging the faithful to receive absolution and the Eucharist in association with anointing. Although, at this stage, the faithful were still allowed to take the oil away to anoint themselves or their friends, they were by this fashion drawn more to seek anointing in church by the priest who had first given them absolution and would afterwards give them the Eucharist. The practice of auricular confession was only in its infancy, customs varied in different areas, but here, at least in embryo, is the practice that later crystallized in the ruling of the Council of Pavia in AD 850[21] that none should be anointed until after they had received absolution and Communion.

This regulation had far-reaching results. The passage in S. James' Epistle[22] links healing and absolution – the sufferer is to receive healing both of body and soul. The increasing association of penance and anointing meant that the latter came to be regarded as itself a ministry to penitents to such an extent that the emphasis was laid upon healing of soul rather than, although not totally excluding, healing of the body. Thus anointing came *ipso facto* into the sphere of the priest's ministry through his authority to absolve penitents, and gradually the earlier custom of taking the oil home for anointing fell into disuse. In the thirteenth century S. Thomas Aquinas reserved the ministry solely to priests partly for this reason, and also because by then anointing had become recognized as one of the seven sacraments of the Church. It was still some time, however, before the custom crystallized into a definite rule.[23]

Rites of anointing

Formal rites of anointing can be traced back to the end of the fifth or early sixth century. The two features, the charge to the Apostles and the reference to James 5 frequently occur in such orders. There are also passages of scripture; in the later rites these usually concern Gospel miracles of healing or some reference to the Holy Spirit; in the earlier rites the choice appears to centre upon the Resurrection. One of the interesting features of the various rites is the survival of the early custom of the Laying on of Hands which in these rites is placed side by side with anointing, some times retaining some of the earlier prayers which originally accompanied the Laying on of Hands.[24]

One of the earliest rites is found in the Spanish *Liber Ordinum*. Among other early examples of anointing in church by a priest are some liturgical fragments of Celtic origin.[25] These belong to a liturgical tradition distinct from either the Roman or the Eastern. In these fragments there is no direct mention of any Laying on of Hands nor any directions as to where the anointing is to be made, but it is reasonable to conclude that practices as early as this follow the custom of anointing the forehead. These rites preserve something of the joyful spontaneity of the early Church; they all end on notes of joy and praise and there are even directions for the sick to sing; 'but if unable to do so the priest will sing for him'. In trying to recapture the mind of the early centuries of the Church these fragments have a valuable contribution to make.[26]

In popular thought, because of the emphasis laid upon the association of anointing with the remission of sins the aspect of physical healing faded into the background and sometimes disappeared altogether. S. Bede, writing more than a hundred years before the Council of Pavia insisted that the remission of sins belonged to the absolution which should precede anointing; but the more the emphasis came to be laid upon the spiritual nature of the healing received the more it came to be thought of as itself a special means of absolution.

Long before the Christian era sickness had been associated in popular Greek and Roman thought with the anger of the gods, and Jewish thought on the subject is reflected in the attitude of Job's 'comforters', or in the question put to Christ concerning the man born blind.[27] An instinctive recognition in man of the close association between sin and sickness can be seen throughout the history of Christian healing, but it does not mean that every theory regarding details and consequences of this has been correct. Often theories have been too individualistic and have overlooked the corporate inheritance both of original sin in the past and communal sin in the contemporary environment; sometimes there has been a lack of proportion over-emphasizing either one or other of the components. The Church has, however, rightly seen the importance of placing any physical ministration within the ministry to the soul.[28] It was not the removal of the physical symptom in isolation, but the wholeness of the personality by the quickening of eternal life in both body and soul through a more vital contact with Christ that constituted the healing the Church sought to minister to the sick.

The close association of sin and sickness, much in popular thought in the Middle Ages, was to come out very prominently in connection with the ministry to the sick. Anointing came to be seen as a supreme means of reconciliation with God, and by the ninth century the faithful were seeking anointing for the remission of sins when on their death-bed. From this custom gradually grew the doctrine that was later to crystallize in Roman theology into the Sacrament of Extreme Unction. As the change of emphasis became generally widespread, church authorities reminded priests to anoint the sick as penitents and to insist upon the Sacrament of Penance in association with it. As anointing was now regarded as itself a penitential sacrament some further elucidation was needed to distinguish it from the Sacrament of Penance which preceded it, and in this way, about the middle of the twelfth century the term 'Extreme Unction' came into use, Peter Lombard (1100–60) being the first to use it in his definition of the seven sacraments. It was not then an official description; that was to follow later. Quite probably all that was meant by 'Extreme' was 'last' in the sense of last of the three anointings associated with the sacraments, the two earlier being at Baptism and Confirmation.[29]

The term 'Extreme' was not always used. 'Solemn', 'Holy' or just simply 'Unction' were frequently found. S. Thomas Aquinas used the word 'Solemn'; at the Council of Trent when the subject received more formal treatment.[30]

The Eastern Church never adopted the term 'Extreme' although when it was used in 1274 at the Council of Lyons their delegates raised no objection to it.

At the Council of Florence in 1439 a ruling was made that: 'Extreme Unction . . . shall not be given except to a sick person whose death is apprehended'; a requirement which has since been considerably modified.[31] It could be administered after unconsciousness and up to four hours after death. The provision for the sick who were not so gravely ill lay in the rite entitled 'Of the Care of the Sick'.

Popular opinion was now regarding this as the last and most solemn sacrament for the remission of sins, and thus the practice grew up of postponing it until the last moment, in much the same way as there were those in the Early Church who postponed Baptism for fear of post-baptismal sin. Thus gradually Extreme Unction came to be regarded as the last sacrament which disposed the soul for glory.[32] There were those who even believed that by Extreme Unction all ties with the world were extinguished, so that if recovery should take place the sufferer must in future renounce the eating of meat and matrimonial relations. This misunderstanding – since authoritatively denied – at one time led people to hesitate to have children anointed, and there were in Europe, even up to the beginning of this century, peasants who thought that one who received Extreme Unction should be left to die. Needless to say this was not the official teaching of the Church, but it shows the extent to which the thought of physical healing had been eclipsed, ignored or even rejected.

For the Eastern Church the spiritual aspect of anointing had also developed. The root meaning of the sacrament was repentance and reconciliation, with healing as a consequence, and because it was for the healing of soul as well as body the faithful were, and still are, able to resort to it for any ills, not only physical. It was and is granted to all without the requirement that the sufferer should be *in articulo mortis*. At the same time, the Eastern Church uses this sacrament for the dying far more than the Western, although not as one of the last rites in the Western sense, but toward healing of soul and body. In the Eastern Church it is administered to those who have lost consciousness, not from fear of their subsequently sinning if the sufferer recovers, but because the power and efficacy of the sacrament can penetrate through the unconscious.

More attention meanwhile was being paid to the spiritual value of suffering. There was less evidence of the Church's power of physical healing, and more emphasis was laid upon sickness as a participation in the sufferings of Christ. The close connection between sin and sickness was stressed; the sufferers were to see in their suffering a school of sanctity, a refining crucible, sent or permitted by God for the soul's health. Those who visited the sick were to exhort them to seek patience, resignation, submission and abandonment rather than release from their pain. This development was to receive increasing emphasis in the following centuries.[33]

One of the consequences of this was a certain form of resignation which led to inertia with regard to the ministry of healing, and also at times to the neglect of the sick by the clergy, relegating ministry to them to the physician, irrespective of their spiritual needs. This was so far from the spirit of Christ that the church had to make regulations obliging the clergy to fulfil their duty.

The Fourth Lateran Council in 1215 insisted that doctors must give priority to the spiritual welfare of their patients and exhort them to seek first the ministry of the Church. Doctors who refused were forbidden entry into the Church until they had made satisfaction. Although the cleavage between medicine and priestcraft may date back to the time of Hippocrates, as far as the Christian Church was concerned this marked a definite stage in a long story of rift and non-cooperation.

The background to all this must not be forgotten: the separation between East and West, the struggle between temporal and spiritual power, between 1378 and 1417 rival claimants for the papacy, and within the church simony, laxity, dissension. It is not surprising under these conditions that there is less evidence of physical healing; even in the third century S. Cyprian was telling the Church that the power of healing was similarly diminished by a weakening of spiritual life.[34] On the other hand, the deep spiritual lives of individual saints and the rise of religious orders during these centuries – often through the inspiration of individual sanctity and vocation – was the leaven hid in the whole which preserved the spiritual life of the church.[35]

During these centuries, when healing by anointing was changing from the practice of the early Church to the definition of the fifteenth century of Unction as the Last Sacrament of Penance, there are very many well attested instances of healing through the prayer and ministry of saints.[36] There were pilgrimages to sacred shrines, invocation of saints, the use of relics.[37] Images in the West, icons in the East had their association with healing; the kings of England and France were exercising the Royal Touch for scrofula.[38] In England, among other shrines, the shrine of Our Lady of Walsingham dating from 1061 was famous for healings that took place until its destruction in 1538. It is now again restored as a famous centre of pilgrimage and healing.

Modern Times (sixteenth to twentieth century)

Already it has been necessary to trace two distinct lines of development in doctrine and practice as a result of the division between East and West. Confronted with the Reformation differences multiply although at the outset there is much in common, and throughout the history of Protestantism there is more agreement in this particular field than appears on the surface.

Luther saw a closer relation between sickness and sin than many of his contemporaries and stressed the diabolic origin of disease. He regarded sickness as symptomatic of spiritual disorder and permitted by God in His goodness for correction and refining. He saw this remedial pain, however intense, as light in comparison with the Passion of Christ endured for the salvation of the sufferer's soul, and he taught patient resignation. At the same time Luther had firm confidence in God's power to heal and did not discourage either medical science, for which he had great respect, nor the prayer of faith, which, he says, will bring healing if God sees it is good for the soul's health. But Luther felt that the more enlightened believers would sometimes see that the spiritual benefits gained through their sickness were so great that they might not desire healing; whereas miracles of healing were for those with less patience and insight, and were to be expected in answer to the prayer of faith.

In connection with Unction Luther claimed that the anointing referred to in *James* 5 was 'if any is sick' not 'if any is dying', and was intended to restore to health; he supported his contention by reference to prayers used in the early Church and still often retained in use, in which healing is definitely sought. He therefore repudiated what he understood to be the Roman teaching of his day on the Sacrament of Extreme Unction, and felt that healing through anointing as practised in apostolic times was a thing of the past. The Canons of the Council of Trent[39] on this subject were partly framed as a reply to this.

Calvin follows much the same line as Luther; he sees many causes of sickness – diabolical, social, hereditary and individual sins – but all within the foreseen will of God to which the sufferer must be resigned; for sickness can be a means of grace for deepening the knowledge of God, a merciful call to repentance, a means of correction and a participation in Christ's sufferings.

In order that the sick should be guided to see this he ordered that nobody should be bedridden for more than three days without notifying the minister who could then instruct and encourage the sufferer.

Calvin accepted medical science as a divine gift not to be despised, but believed that God could heal directly without any intermediary. He held similar views to Luther about Extreme Unction and said that if the Church really believed, as he did not, that there was a healing for physical ills in Extreme Unction it was cruel to leave it until too late.

Most Protestants thought as did Luther and Calvin about Extreme Unction. In general they believed in anointing as practised in the early Church for any who were sick, not only for the dying; a view not different in general principle from the teaching that followed from the Council of Trent. There is a famous exhortation to the clergy of his diocese by the Roman Catholic bishop of Cleremont, Massillon[40] who suggested that it was profanation of this sacrament to leave it so late that it would be unlikely to be of much use. He may have been thinking primarily of the spiritual rather than the physical benefit, but there is no ambiguity about the position of Pope Benedict XIV[41] fifteen years later when he reminded the faithful that this sacrament had been ordained not only for the soul but also for the physical healing of those seriously ill; i.e. he clearly pointed out that it was the sick and not only those at the point of death who were envisaged; and in the twentieth century the following extract from a Roman Catholic abbot is equally clear:

'In spite of the name of Extreme Unction ... and notwithstanding the almost universal belief, it must not be supposed that the Sacrament is intended by the Church only as the immediate and final preparation for death. It is in reality the Sacrament of the sick, the anointing of the sick, the object of which is to cure both soul and body; it can be received more than once in a lifetime. It is want of faith which makes Catholics put off receiving it until all hope of recovery is past, and the sick person, doomed to an inevitable and speedy death, is no longer in a state to respond to the sacramental action. For that last hour, for that final struggle, there is yet another rite ... the Recommendation of the Departing Soul.'[42]

Since that was written the position has been made much clearer. The present liturgical revision is more evidently in line with the teaching and practice of the early Church.[43]

The Church of England at the Reformation preserved in the Visitation of the Sick a rite of Holy Anointing for those who desired to avail themselves of it. This was in the first Prayer Book of Edward VI in 1549, but in the 1552 and subsequent versions it no longer appeared, the reason given being that the rite had fallen into disuse, was only an optional rite and could therefore be removed as obsolete. Not until the twentieth century would it again find a place in the Anglican Church. Resolution 73c of the

1958 Lambeth Conference urges that a chief aim of prayer book revision should be to further that recovery of the worship of the primitive Church which was the aim of the compilers of the first prayer books of the Church of England. In the committee report on the subject of the ministry to the sick recommendation was made for the inclusion, after certain new rubrics and directives, of seven additional elements, amongst which are a ritual for the Laying on of Hands and for Holy Anointing. The latter steps still wait to be implemented; meanwhile a Form of Unction and the Laying on of Hands approved by the Convocations of Canterbury and York in 1935 is in use, subject to diocesan sanction.[44, 45]

In the eighteenth century Bengel (1687–1752) the Lutheran theologian in Germany, and in England Wesley (1703–1791) both recognized anointing as the great, regular means of healing in the Church. The latter interpreted the passage in James 5, 15 'if he have committed sin...' as referring to any sin which was the cause of the particular illness for which anointing was administered.

A general background of theological differences influenced a Protestant move from sacramental healing to something more direct and individual. The sacramental, the powers handed down by apostolic succession, were not always appreciated. Although in some cases, as in those just mentioned, anointing still took a prominent place, a new emphasis came to be placed upon gifts bestowed upon individuals. Thus the charismatic ministry, the prayer of faith, the literal acceptance and claiming of scriptural promises, whilst not absent from Catholic teaching were more specifically characteristic of Protestant movements. Also, a larger place than many have realized was given by them to the importance of corporate prayer. Much attention was paid to the power of the individual prayer of faith but there was also the praying congregation, the recognition that the whole body of the faithful was behind the one who ministered to the sick. Bengel expressed this very clearly when he said that when the Elders of the Church pray it is as if the whole force of faith of the whole Christian body were present.

Both Protestants and Catholics agreed upon the close connection between sin and sickness, and upon the value of sickness as an awakening to repentance, moving man to a greater depen-

dence upon God as a means of growth in holiness. Being permitted for the soul's healing by God, who, as Fenelon put it 'only
cuts to cure' – a phrase any surgeon would appreciate! Both
stress patience, resignation and submission, but there is a very
wide range to this teaching; at its best, in a positive form, it can
be seen in De Caussade's *Abandonment to Divine Providence*,[46] but
at the other extreme is negative quietism. It was not always realized that God's will, to which submission was taught, might
well be a will to heal and that he was waiting for the sufferer, in
positive cooperation, to stretch out the hand of faith to receive
this gift of healing. There were, too, those who knew the truth
that great redemptive power flows from uniting personal suffering with the Passion of Christ. The lives of many saints have witnessed to this, but those same lives who pressed the thorns so
close that they exuded balm[47] were in the forefront of those who
worked to ameliorate and heal.

However great the truth of the goodness to which sickness can
be turned, it may not be altogether out of place to see in some of
the teaching at this time a rationalization, unintentional and
unconscious, to account for the decrease of healing work in the
preceding centuries. This finds support from the fact that times
of revival were accompanied by a steadily increasing return of
healing work, and where the Church was vitally alive, even in
the Middle Ages, a ministry of healing sometimes very close to
that recorded in the New Testament can be found, for example in
the lives of the saints or in some of the religious orders. The con-
versation between Bishop Butler and Wesley in the eighteenth
century illustrates this: 'The days have gone when the Church
could say with S. Peter, "Silver and gold have I none"', with the
reply 'The days have gone when the Church could say to the
lame man "Take up thy bed and walk"'. In the following century
the case is put by the Curé d'Ars: 'God is always Almighty, he
can always do miracles, and he would do them as of old, but
faith is lacking'. It was said of him: 'M. le Curé did not allow for
any "if" or "but" with the Good God – when one asks a grace
and puts conditions on it one is sure to obtain nothing at all'.[48]

The twentieth century approach to healing is in the context of
technology and rapidly increasing scientific knowledge. More
than two centuries have passed since Hume and the Deists
sought to discount the miraculous. Modern scientific know-

ledge, for example of psychology or magnetism, may account for some of the phenomena of healing, especially at times of revival or under the influence of strong suggestion, but this does not by any means cover the whole ground. God comes to man through the things of mind and sense but to analyse how a process of healing works is not the last word, it neither rules out the divine factor whence the process may be set in motion, nor does it close the door to more direct divine activity beyond the measurement of man. The author of nature can do what is beyond nature and Christ taught that the prayer of faith can set in operation some of these supernatural laws.

Not much attention was paid from the latter part of the Middle Ages until the seventeenth century to the charisma of healing. The general consensus of opinion was that the ministry had long since ceased; there were occasional instances of it but they were regarded as exceptional. There definitely appears however to be evidence of a return of this ministry of the healing work of the saints, for example S. Francis Xavier (1506–1552).

In sharp contrast to this is the emphasis placed from the middle of the seventeenth century on the continued presence of these gifts. With the revival of spiritual life in many quarters at this time the presence of healing and evidence of charisma became increasingly manifest. George Fox the Quaker (1624–1691) was certain that he had received the gift of healing, and he may be regarded as the forerunner of all Protestant movements in which this revival is found. Edward Irving[49] (1792–1834) said that the absence of gifts was like the absence of flowers in winter – spring would follow.

Protestant denominations were too many and too varied for detailed consideration; there would be few, if any, that did not witness to at least some degree of healing work and it was often a prominent feature. Many leading figures in the revival of this ministry felt that miracles were but accidentals to the main task of evangelization, signs which were not the essence of the Gospel, and in some cases they tried to prevent such occurrences being publicized.[50] Nevertheless, all had confidence in God's power to heal, a power that was still available when medical skill could do no more.[51] Ami Bost, who has been called 'the flower of Protestant charity' pointed out that if God granted such supernatural gifts as piety, charity and humility it was not unreasonable to seek also lesser gifts such as those of health. His son Jean was the founder of the hospital at La Force.

In general the attitude to the medical profession was one of respect and cooperation, but there are various qualifications to this. Wesley was not the only one who felt that the patient's faith might become diverted from God to the doctor; others, more extreme, felt faith would be so undermined that they discouraged recourse to medical help, but this is not representative of the main Protestant attitude. Blumhardt (a German pastor in the mid-nineteenth century) felt it was foolish to reject the doctor's help, but he denounced the inability of the medical profession of his day to see the close connection between sin and sickness.

A theologian of the Swiss Reformed Church, A. R. Vinet (1797–1847), regarded the care of the sick as the most important duty of pastors. Many homes and centres of healing were opened during these centuries and the numbers healed were considerable.[52] In the last hundred years there has been a marked increase in the number of such healing centres and this is a steadily growing phenomenon.

In the Roman Church orders and congregations for the care of the sick sprang up and flourished in the seventeenth century and after such as those inspired by S. Francis de Sales and Mme. de Chantal; S. Vincent de Paul, S. Camillus de Lellis.[53]

The eighteenth century saw a great increase in the rise of hospitals, for example eight of the larger London hospitals were founded between 1719 and 1765.[54]

At all periods of her history the help of the Church Triumphant has been recognized, and above all Mary, Queen of Heaven. Many were the shrines and places associated with her. When belief in miracles of healing was returning in Protestant circles she herself took the initiative in the Roman Church in a still greater healing movement, greater not in the numerical sense – many and well attested as the numbers of these physical cures have been – but in the sense that she recalled the faithful to the radical way of healing. There were two notable instances of this in the nineteenth century. The first was in 1846 at La Salette, a village in the Alps near Grenoble, when she appeared to children. Her message was a promise of divine mercy after repentance.[55]

Twelve years later the same message was given in Lourdes in

the words 'Prayer and penance'. Were they an echo of her son's words: 'This kind can come forth by nothing, but by prayer and fasting'?[56]

A third instance was in 1917. Although the threefold message from this experience at Fatima was expressed in the terminology of the Roman Church,[57] the message is the same, i.e. prayer and penance.

These centres are now places of pilgrimage, especially Lourdes where Our Lady of Lourdes draws the vast concourse of pilgrims, not only to find there physical relief, which frequently is the case,[58] but also that they may see how they themselves may both be more radically healed and share in the redemptive, healing work of Christ for mankind. Many of those who go on pilgrimage to Lourdes, if they do not receive actual physical healing, are strengthened and helped by some glimpse of the meaning of this redemptive work, and give themselves to this way of healing as S. Bernadette gave herself as a victim of love, and found thus a perfect fulfilment of her life and its meaning and destiny.

At the same time as the apparitions at Lourdes the healing power of a life of prayer and penance was being witnessed in the village of Ars, where the whole life of the curé was one uninterrupted healing ministry, primarily the healing of souls, as can be seen from his long hours in the confessional, but powerful too for physical cures. By 1855 the number of pilgrims to Ars was estimated at 20,000 a year.

At the end of the nineteenth century S. Thérèse of Lisieux understood this message and, a great sufferer herself – as was S. Bernadette – followed the same path; her healing work made manifest in a great harvest both of physical cures and other blessings.

Another outstanding example, still nearer to the present time, is the life of prayer and penance of Padre Pio at San Giovanni Rotundo, where pilgrims from all over the world were drawn for help and healing, and which since his death remains a healing centre. Not all the journalistic accounts of his healing work can be accepted at their face value but there can be no doubt that some of these miracles can stand the test of the strictest scientific investigation.[59]

These instances illustrate the close connection between sin

and sickness; life and love meet, by love the way of penance is followed and leads to life physical and spiritual, as also to the very fount of life Himself from whom all healing flows.

Not only in the Roman Church but also elsewhere the ministry of healing was receiving fresh impetus. In the early twentieth century new interest was aroused by the world-wide missions of J. M. Hickson and others, the repercussions of which are seen at the present time in the organizations, homes of healing, and intercession groups which have sprung up both in England and overseas. In the Anglican Church as in the Roman Church since the restoration of the Shrine of Our Lady of Walsingham an ever increasing number of pilgrims visit and receive great healing blessings there.

In the Eastern Church the ministry continues with unbroken continuity; there has always been available the sacrament of anointing, and there have also been individuals whose ministry clearly indicated that they possessed a charisma of healing. These were to be found amongst the Staretzi, generally layfolk who became monks and reached a degree of great spiritual maturity under the guidance of the Holy Spirit. In general they were neither great theologians nor ordained priests, but were powerful men of prayer, such as S. Seraphim of Sarov (1759–1833) who after thirty-seven years of life as a hermit was called from this strict seclusion to become a Staretz. When he was healing a desperately sick man (Mantourov) he said to him: 'Through the grace given to me I treat you medically', and added 'It is not my business to make men die or live . . . It is the business of the one Saviour who listens to prayer'. Of another Staretz, nearer the present time, S. John of Kronstadt, Forbes Robinson, preaching in Christ's College, Cambridge in 1900 said: 'There lives today a saintly man in an island near St Petersburg who probably has more power in prayer than any man now living. He has the reputation through the vast districts of Russia of working miracles.'[60]

In addition to the heterogeneous multiplicity of Christian sects claiming a healing ministry, there have grown up other bodies that have their own approach to healing work, which may or may not have some interest in Christianity, and whose methods have sometimes been confused with Christian healing.

Christian Science has found a way of thought and mental

training by which healings can, in some cases, be effected. It is similar in many ways to the Gnosticism met with by the early Church. Through the denial of the reality of matter it denies, by implication, the reality of the Incarnation.

Spiritualist bodies also have their healing ministry, but the direct faith in Christ which is integral to Christian healing is not necessarily required either of the spirits invoked or of the mediums through whom they work.

There is all the difference in the world between the spiritualist use of mediums and the invocation of saints in the Christian Church. The latter rests upon the truth of the Communion of Saints in the Body of Christ indivisible by death. The saints are not invoked as healers but as intercessors; they have been known to be powerful in prayer during their earthly life, and just as friends ask the help of the prayers of those still on earth, so prayer to Christ for his healing is asked from those in the nearer presence of God. This can be a great encouragement to any group of intercessors and will help them to realize that they are not alone in their prayer, but are acting as a cell of the whole corporate Body of the Church both militant and triumphant in lifting up to God those to whom the Church is called to minister.

There is no need to deny that these other bodies claiming to heal may produce some degree of beneficial results, but it is pathetic that such practices draw many away from the Church to seek healing elsewhere; this is due, in part, to inadequate teaching and ministry by the traditional churches. Although much is being done to remedy the situation, there is need of renewal so that this ministry which is integral to the Gospel be revived again in all its power in every church and congregation.

Chapter notes

1. In the fourth century the use of sacred relics became officially recognized.
2. AD 338–401.
3. See S. Athanasius, S. Gregory Nazianus, S. Ambrose, S. Martin of Tours, the monks of the Egyptian desert.
4. AD 315–86.
5. AD 540–604.
6. AD 480–543.
7. + AD 605.

8. AD 672–734.
9. AD 378–448.
10. AD 605–42.
11. AD 636–87.
12. See p. 40.
13. Pope 402–17.
14. Ephraim mentions this rite in the East *c.* AD 370 (see Sermon 46 *Adv. Haer.*).
15. See p. 60.
16. See p. 48.
17. S. Chrysostom (AD 347–407) mentions this custom.
18. e.g. S. Genevieve *c.* AD 422–500.
19. See S. John Damascene AD 675–749.
20. See *Canons of Laodicea* C4 and S. Cyril of Alexandria C5.
21. Canon VIII.
22. 5. 14–16.
23. From as early as the fourth or fifth century it became the custom to recite the seven penitential psalms during the anointing.
24. The rubrics about the Laying on of Hands vary considerably. In at least one instance not only the priests and ministers present are all to lay their hands on the sufferer but also the laity (see Codex Eligii – mid-ninth century). The rites include various other symbols such as the Sign of the Cross, the invocation of the Name either of Christ or the Trinity, the use of Holy Water. The rites differ as to which parts of the body are to be anointed; in the earliest rites it was only on the forehead; later, in general the organs of sense are mentioned, but in two similar rites about AD 900 special emphasis is laid upon anointing the parts where the pain is most acute. (Codex Eligii and S. Gatian of Tours)
25. Three fragments, namely: 1. An Irish fragment attributed to Dimma who lived in the seventh century. 2. A fragment written in a ninth century hand, ascribed to Mulling who was Bishop of Ferns in the seventh century. 3. A fragment from Deer in Aberdeenshire. The date of this extant fragment is prior to 1130 but the original was probably considerably earlier. *The Book of Deer* belonged to the monks of the monastery founded at Deer by S. Columba in the sixth century; this fragment probably represents part of their liturgy for the sick in its early form.
26. For these Celtic rites see R. C. West, *Western Liturgies*, also F. E. Warren, *Liturgy and Ritual of the Celtic Church*. A valuable collection of early rites of anointing and also much useful material concerning the healing ministry in these early centuries is to be found in R. M. Woolley, D. D. *Exorcism and the Healing of the Sick*, published in 1932 by SPCK for the Church Historical Association.

27. John 9. 2.
28. cf. Goethe: 'It is the spirit which builds the body'.
29. It could mean 'Last' in the sense of the last of the three sacraments at the anointing, the others being Absolution and Communion, but this does not seem to have been suggested as an explanation, and before the Council of Pavia in 850 anointing was placed before Communion.
30. See p. 71.
31. See p. 66.
32. This view was supported by S. Albert the Great, S. Bonaventura, S. Thomas Aquinas and others. Duns Scotus went so far as to ignore any possibility of healing, and he recommended, in order to ensure that the sufferer should not sin again, that Unction should not be administered until he had lost consciousness.
33. S. Thomas Aquinas (1225–74) said that Unction did not heal the body unless the healing was for the soul's benefit, but that it would help other remedies through the spiritual joy it conferred. (*Summa* XXX 2).
34. cf. p. 40.
35. Famous among such orders were the Cistercians (eleventh century), Carthusians (twelfth century), Dominicans and Franciscans (thirteenth century) and for the release of over a million captives the Order of Our Lady of Ransom and the Order of the Trinitarians (both thirteenth century).
36. For example S. Bernard (1090–1153), S. Hugh of Lincoln (1140–1200), S. Francis of Assisi (1181–1226), S. Roch (1295–1327)
37. S. Vincent Ferrer (1350–1419).
38. A practice subsequently defended by the Council of Trent. According to tradition the kings of England and France had the exclusive right to be anointed at their coronation with pure chrism, not with the sacred oil normally used for coronations. Belief in the healing power granted to these kings seems to be associated with this. Evidence for this practice dates from the thirteenth century in France and the fourteenth in England, although it was thought to originate in the fifth century in France and the eleventh in England. The last recorded in England was in the reign of Queen Anne; in France the practice continued a little longer. By the reign of Charles II the number of those seeking permits to receive it was over 100,000.
39. See p. 96.
40. 1663–1742.
41. 1675–1758.
42. *Liturgical Prayer: its History and Spirit.* Cabrol, p. 274. The rite for the Recommendation of a Departing Soul is a very ancient one; in its

present form it goes back to the ninth century and contains some prayers that belong to the Primitive Church.

43. See further p. 78.
44. In the Revised Scottish and the American Prayer Book of 1929 and the Alternative Book of Occasional Offices authorized for the provinces of S. Africa provision is made for Holy Anointing.
45. The form in use in the C of E may be obtained from the Guild of Health, 26 Queen Anne Street, London W1M 9LB (10p).
46. 1751.
47. 'Thorns give forth balm and the Cross sweetness. But we must squeeze the thorns in our hands, and press the Cross to our heart, to make them distil the fragrance which is within them.' The Curé d'Ars, cited in his *Life* by Monnin, Ch. 19.
48. See *Life of the Curé* by Trochu, Ch. 27.
49. The Irvingites placed much emphasis upon the work of the Holy Spirit and believed firmly in the charismata which should be used as in Apostolic times.
50. e.g. in the case of Zinzendorf the Moravian (cir. 1738).
51. cf. Charles Cullis, a doctor in Boston, U.S.A. (cir. 1873) who was especially noted for the healing of tuberculosis and cancer.
52. A notable centre was the Moravian one at Herrnhut.
53. See also: the sixteenth century Jesuit Order; one condition of entry was a readiness to care for the sick. At the beginning of the eighteenth century the Daughters of Wisdom founded by S. Grignon de Montfort.
54. Westminster 1719, Guys 1734, Middlesex 1745, Lock 1746, Queen Charlotte 1752, Royal 1757, London 1740, Westminster Lying In 1765.
55. Some doubt was at first cast upon the children's story but it was subsequently accepted as authentic, and La Salette has become a place of pilgrimage witnessing many cures through the 'Virgin of the Alps'.
56. Mark 9. 29 A.V. If the words 'and fasting' are not part of the original text as is suggested by some early documents, they still represent what was believed to be the purport of Christ's reply. 'Do penance' is the Douai translation of Mark 1, 15 and parallel passages. The varied versions mean much the same thing in practice, cf. Luke 3, 8.
57. a) penance, b) recitation of the Rosary, c) devotion to the Immaculate Heart of Mary.
58. Physical benefits are not limited to the few healings that are claimed to be miraculous.
59. For example the healing in 1947 of Gemma di Giordi aged 7, blind from birth. It was considered by the medical profession impossible that she should regain her sight. There was a healing similar to this

at Lourdes in 1908 of Mme Biré which was subjected to the usual seven searching tests required by the Lourdes Medical Bureau before it was officially accepted as miraculous.

60. S. Barsanuphius, a sixth-century Staretz in Palestine was famed for raising the dead, casting out demons, curing incurable diseases and many other miracles. He said: 'No one can be cured without God. He who gives himself up to the art of healing must surrender himself to the name of God, and God will send him help'. For further details of the Eastern Church see p. 98ff.

6

The present day

The foregoing outline has bridged the gap between the primitive Church and the present day. In Part I some consideration was given to the relation of the modern background to present practice. It now remains to consider how any misunderstandings, deviations or misrepresentations noted in these intervening years can be corrected today, and also to consider the legacy of positive guidance, based on experience through the centuries, the wisdom of which needs to be appreciated as providing necessary safeguards for the preservation of both doctrine and practice.

The most significant contribution has arisen in connection with anointing. The Second Vatican Council, in the fourth amendment to Ch. 3 of the Schema on the Liturgy, changes the title from 'Extreme Unction' on the grounds that it is not only a sacrament for those in danger of death but for all those for whom sickness or old age constitutes an initial step in that direction. A new rite entitled *'The Anointing of the Sick'* was drawn up and authorized for the Roman Church in 1972. In this is a prayer that those anointed[1] may be freed from pain and illness and made well again in body, mind and spirit. The sacrament is intended for those who are seriously ill or in the weakness of old age, and should not be left too late; there are circumstances in which it may be repeated, and it may be administered to children if they are old enough to understand what it means.

This corrects any misunderstandings or ambiguities in the past. It recognizes that sickness can be a great means of union with the passion and death of Christ for the good of the whole people of God; at the same time attention is drawn to the duty of fighting courageously against it and earnestly seeking healing.

This is a clear corrective to the negative state of resignation and is in line with both psychological knowledge and the preventive and remedial work of the social services.

In the current liturgical revision the concern for a closer correspondence with the worship and prayers of the primitive Church is an important contribution. The modern Western Mass for the Sick definitely prays quite unconditionally in the collect that the sick 'may be restored to health'.[2]

Today misunderstandings in relation to the medical profession are being replaced by cooperation and understanding. There is now opportunity for clergy and ordinands to have short courses to gain insight into the working of hospitals for both physical and mental cases. There is also an appreciation by the church of psychological factors about which the medical profession is rightly concerned, while on the part of the latter there has been an increasing recognition of the role of the church in serving the spiritual needs of the patient: they now have a voice on the councils working for the revival of this ministry. The gulf between the language of theology and that of an exact science such as medicine is not easy to bridge, especially with the increase of specialization, but there are those who, by qualifying both as priest and doctor, are in this sense bilingual; moreover Christianity known and experienced is not the sole prerogative of the theologian.

While separate confessions rightly have their own organizations for the direction and regulation of their work,[3] a great impetus to cooperation has been given by the present ecumenical movement. The breaking down of barriers which have been divisive in the past allows for an interchange which is mutually enriching; much valuable work is now being done by cooperative efforts of ecumenical organizations.[4] The inspiration of the late Archbishop Temple in founding the Churches' Council for Health and Healing has provided in this country a valuable instrument for cooperation, study and witness. It is open to all members and associate members of the British Council of Churches and to the Roman Catholic Church and it has links with the great medical and nursing colleges and organizations.[5]

Within the framework of this Council it should be possible, allowing for the liberty of interpretation of different confessions, for a strong lead to be given both in sound theology and wise, disciplined regularization. In addition to this centralized body there are other groups working in a similar way, such as the Institute of Religion and Medicine.

Not only in Great Britain, but in all five continents, the work is growing, as for example through the International Order of S. Luke centred in America, the aim of which is:

'To bring back the teaching of Our Lord Jesus Christ as set forth in the Gospels and in the Acts of the Apostles to their rightful place within the Christian Church, through constructive teaching and through cooperation with those clergy, physicians and psychologists who have discovered in the Divine Being the source and secret of wholeness.'

The Universal Guild of Divine Healing in Canada aims:

'To labour for the restoration of the healing ministry of Jesus Christ to the Church . . . to build and encourage prayer groups for the purpose of study and intercession for the sick . . . to pray and work for close cooperation between the Church and the medical profession . . . to use the sacramental gifts of the Church as effective means of grace . . . .'

Side by side with these developments, and to some extent following from them, is a growing recognition of the need for study; and an increasing number of parishes, congregations and groups take an active part in this work.

The legacy of positive guidance based on experience through the centuries has much to contribute.

Early in her history the Church found the need for regulation. The free and easy practices of the first days when numbers were comparatively small were unsuited to the greater world-wide Church. This needs to be remembered by enthusiasts for a return to the primitive Church. Whilst rigidity is out of place, sheep need shepherds endowed by the Holy Spirit and commissioned by the Good Shepherd, and also a fold which protects from the ever vigilant lions and wolves.

As a result of decrees of earlier councils the visitation of the Sick is obligatory; they are not to be left to the doctors without help from the church. To heal the sick – not just visit but heal – is still implicit in the charge given to bishops at their consecration.

The oil for anointing is still, in the West, blessed by the bishop in his cathedral on the Thursday in Holy Week. It has been the custom in both East and West to recite the penitential psalms in connection with anointing, and although this custom may be modified the note of penitence is still retained, as well as the association with the Eucharist.

The experience of the Church has led to important regulation concerning exorcism. The minor order which began in the third century in connection with pre-baptismal exorcisms ceased to exist in that form a few years ago, but the power of exorcism is included in the special grace conferred at ordination to the priesthood, and for lesser forms of exorcism, for example blessing of holy water or houses – where it is in constant use.

When it was a matter of coming to grips with greater forms of evil the dangers of the free and easy use of early times was recognized, and it was found to be important that there should be careful supervision and regularization of this practice. There is today in the West a formal rite for the exorcism of demons which is prefaced by a number of very wise admonitions for the one who is to perform the exorcism. These regulations, based on those which date back as far as the fourth century, direct that the more solemn exorcisms may only be performed by a bishop, or in some cases by a priest authorized by him.[6] Today it is also required that the bishop should be satisfied that there is no psychopathological or other tenable diagnosis before coming to the conclusion that the case is one requiring exorcism. The notable forces of evil present in the world today have drawn attention to the subject of exorcism more than was the case previously, especially in the West. The present exploration of the paranormal can open the door to evils which it is the concern of the church to combat; this is particularly true when occult practices are undertaken, which in their prevalence today present a situation not dissimilar from that which confronted the early Church.

These legacies from the past, together with the many other contributing factors in the modern background, some of which were noted in Part I, provide both an encouraging indication of what is already being attempted and a guideline for future advance. This is the setting in which the challenge of the Introduction can be faced.[7]

Chapter notes

1. On forehead and usually also on the palms of the hands. The revised provisional rite issued by the Roman Catholic Church is No. 4 of 5 booklets published by Mayhew-McCrimmon (35p each); the other 4 booklets are 1) *Communion of the Sick.* 2) *Visiting the Sick.* 3) *Mass in the home of the Sick.* 5) *Readings for the Sick.*

2. So does the petition for the sick in the Liturgy for Good Friday, see also prayers found in some of the ancient ceremonies such as Candlemas and the Blessing of the Palms in Holy Week, and also the collect used for the commemoration of the B.V.M.

3. For the Anglican Church the Guild of S. Raphael.

4. Among ecumenical guilds are the Guild of Health, Divine Healing (Mission,) the Burrswood International Fellowship.

5. The present number of member churches represents approximately 25 denominations in addition to the Christian groups working in this field and the representatives of medical and other health professional bodies. The address is St Marylebone Parish Church, Marylebone Rd., NW1, 5LT.

6. In 1604 *Canon 74 of the Convocation of Canterbury* forbade a parish priest without episcopal licence by fasting and prayer to cast out any devil or devils under pain of deposition from the ministry. This canon was made because of the abuse of exorcism.

7. See the Findings of a Commission convened by the Bp of Exeter entitled *Exorcism* – by Petitpierre – SPCK 1972 (50p) also A Report '*Deliverance and Healing*' by a group appointed by the Archbishop of York for study in the York diocese and elsewhere – may be obtained from The Guild of S. Raphael, St Marylebone Parish Church, Marylebone Road, London NW1 5LT (30p), or The Diocesan Office, 4 Minster Yard, York, YO1 2JE, 50p post free.

Part 3

Renewal

1

Facing the challenge

Christ called his followers to something impossible for natural man, as impossible as for a camel to go through the eye of a needle.

Salt and leaven were terms he used, ingredients essentially different from that with which they are to be mixed; they are meant to be potent – a little goes a long way. He expected them to do 'more than others' and to be 'perfect as your Heavenly Father is perfect'; a perfection only possible in a life motivated by the Spirit of the Heavenly Father, through a life lived in a new dimension inaugurated by the Incarnation. The baptized enters eternal life here and now, and can become so impregnated with this life that it can flow through him to others. He becomes a member of an organism which exists to be the extension of the Incarnation through which Christ continues his work that includes healing, radical healing – wholeness – both for individuals and ultimately for the world.

It should be second nature for the Christian to be a channel of life and healing, not by any superimposed culture or self-conscious effort, but by being 'supernaturally natural' according to his regenerate nature. In his work for healing he will be co-operating not only with fellow Christians but with agnostics and other non-Christian colleagues, and will do the ordinary outward and visible things that others do, but ideally there will be an inner, spiritual depth which will give significance to his efforts. Doors are open today for the Church to 'confirm the Word with signs following'; but compared with the primitive Church what can be said of the magnetic power that draws those in need?

Not only is the Christian different from the world, but

Christianity itself is revolutionary; history shows that its impact on the world has been tremendous. 'These people who have been turning the world upside down'[1] was how the Thessalonians described them. This revolution is not primarily a material one, but one in which individuals are radically changed by the spiritual dynamic of Christ and who believe that ultimately, by the leavening impact of the Kingdom of God, society and the world will be transformed.

This is a time of unprecedented opportunity, there is a swing of the pendulum from materialism towards the spiritual and a real hunger and thirst for God. The Church has the answer to these needs, yet many, seeking a meaning of life, search for it in other directions, particularly in Eastern mysticism, whilst all the time it is on their own doorstep in the Christian faith. This is not to devalue the contribution of Eastern religions. We, in the West, 'have no time to stand and stare', and these religions have preserved the stillness and deep silence in which the spiritual is apprehended; they have valuable techniques of contemplation and, particularly in the great religions, something of the true revelation of God; but only the Christian can claim to see 'the glory of God in the face of Jesus Christ' – God Incarnate whom to know is Eternal Life.

This turning elsewhere for a revelation of God is an indication that those outside – and often within – the Church, do not understand what Christianity has to offer. Some may feel that any power it once had has gone, others may recognize that there is something in it which they only vaguely understand, many, recognizing the divine in all creation, fail to appreciate the distinctive nature of Christianity; yet it was said of John the Baptist that 'of all the children born of woman, there is no one greater than John; yet the least in the Kingdom of God is greater than he is'.[2] Similarly, the answer to Nicodemus about regeneration is unambiguous.[3]

There must inevitably be some degree of structure, and trustees who, as custodians of the faith, are responsible to see that it is duly and faithfully handed down from generation to generation, but this is only the outward shell, one aspect of the whole, and it is impossible to consider more than the mere externals of Christian healing in this material context.

For some people this is the only aspect of the Church they see, they think of it in terms of an organization, admission to which is by 'a ceremony called baptism'. (The more ignorant speak of 'having the infant done' as if it meant something on a par with vaccination!) Others only enter a church for weddings, harvest festivals and funerals. This is in marked contrast to the practice of the early Church with its austere, prolonged and careful preparation of catechumens who, in days of persecution, might at any moment be called upon to die for their faith and yet at great risk would not fail to gather together regularly every Lord's Day to worship in the Christian Eucharist.

This may be one of the reasons why in some quarters people regard the Church as insipid instead of inspiring, lifeless instead of virile, archaic instead of progressive. They have not realized that within, and probably beyond the boundaries of the organization is the organism, the Body through which Christ continues his healing work, and through which the seeker can not only find God but also be united to Him.[4] Today the Church is realizing the need to correct the superficial approach and is concerned about ways and means to ensure that the true meaning of Christian initiation is appreciated.

Another factor contributing to this state of affairs may be the substitution of 'doing' for 'being'. External activities are both good and necessary in their right place, but not at the expense of the spiritual from which they should spring, and upon which they depend for real effectiveness. Conferences, committees, lectures, fund-raising efforts, all kinds of social service and many other good works – not to mention the time consuming use of radio and television – all create the illusion that time is shorter than in former days, in spite of the fact that for many technology has lessened working hours. The Church needs to be outgoing and has her contribution to make to social and political life but this, to be effective, must spring from resources of a deep spiritual nature.

There is a great deal of talk about religion, the subject is often studied at a high intellectual level, and sound, scholarly work has been done to meet the need for Christian revelation to be seen against today's background. But it is possible to carry this so far that Christ is bypassed by metaphysics, so that textual criticism and historical analysis may cast doubt upon the underlying truth of the gospel, and a psychological study of S. Paul miss the spiritual import of his letters. If one rich in material wealth can hardly enter the Kingdom, how much harder for one rich in intellectual gifts unless he is also filled with the spirit of wisdom and can stoop to the lowliness that entry demands. 'I bless you, Father, Lord of heaven and of earth, for hiding these things from the learned and the clever and revealing them to mere children'.[5]

Even to the Jews with their rich spiritual heritage that paved the way for the Incarnation, Christ could say: 'You study the scriptures, believing that in them you have eternal life ... and yet you refuse to come to me for life!'[6] It is here, in coming to the contemporary Christ that the keynote to Christian healing is sounded – and nowhere else.

When the spiritual life is starved, awe and worship give place to an easygoing familiarity with God which, while not intentionally irreverent, can be shallow and miss the vision of God known to the mystics.[7] Prayers such as 'My God who am I and who art thou' and the Jesus Prayer of the Eastern Church nourish the life at depth – or one may think of S. Francis of Assisi spending the night in prayer, simply saying 'My God and my all' – a splendid Christian mantra!

> 'Tis ye, 'tis your estrangéd faces,
> That miss the many-splendoured thing.[8]

All these considerations, whilst they are of general importance for Christianity, are directly relevant to the sphere of Christian healing which, too often, has been taken out of its context and put in some watertight compartment.

This is only one side of the picture which needs to be taken into account in facing the challenge described in the Introduction. There are many encouraging signs of an awareness of weakening factors and of progress towards their removal, and there is today throughout the whole world a much greater strength in the Church than her critics realize. Countless numbers of faithful souls are witnessing by their lives, often of heroic sacrifice, to the glory and power of their faith; they are the salt of the earth. In areas of persecution the blood of multitudes of martyrs is still the seed of the Church and already there are many signs of this sacrifice bearing fruit. There is a world-wide wave of spiritual renewal which is bringing fresh vitality into churches and congregations, and in these the ministry of healing is finding its proper place.

The revival of this ministry has come partly through the work of individual pioneers who form the focus of little groups who turn to them for ministration instead of finding the help they need within their own parish or congregation. This has its dangers. The impression may be left that this ministry is extra to the normal life of the Church; the individual may be drawn away from regular worship in his own church and may, unconsciously, receive teaching on lines other than that of the particular church to which he belongs. Whilst it is true that these 'healers' have generally speaking been doing necessary and good pioneer work in their way, the warning in Matthew 24, 24 must not be overlooked. It is not prodigies but wholeness for both body and soul that constitutes Christian healing; this truth is best realized when the healing ministry takes place as part of the whole spiritual stream of life within the particular worshipping body to which the sufferer belongs.

The most practical and necessary development, if sound teaching and practice are to be maintained, is for each church or congregation to have its own healing ministry as part of its regular life; training for this having been provided in the theological colleges or by some central body. The ministry should include anointing and the Laying on of Hands as a regular part of the minister's work, he being supported by the laity who will surround with love and prayer their fellow worshipper in his need, and show their sympathy and care in tactful, unobtrusive involvement and in understanding ways of helping both the sufferer and his family.

There should arise no question as to whether the resulting healing was the result of priestly ministrations or the faith of the praying congregation, or the knowledge and skill of doctor or nurse. Yet just as body and soul are one so all who put their trust in God – whether to inspire the diagnosis, to guide the surgeon's knife or to create healing in some sphere beyond the skill of the scientist – all owe the results not to individual faith but to the corporate, mutually supporting, outreaching hand of faith that receives God's answer to their prayer.

This does not mean that everyone, indiscriminately, will receive the specific form of healing expected. Christian healing is not magic in which man seeks that God will do what he wants, but rather in it man recognizes the boundless love, compassion and wisdom of God, and gladly puts himself unreservedly into God's hands for him to achieve a wholeness greater than his limited knowledge can understand. Christ did not come to create a psychosomatic utopia; wholeness for the Christian is not bounded by this life and healing may begin at a very deep level and may take more than the span of earthly life to complete. One of the great values of the 'if'[9] clause is that it clarifies the distinction between magic where man seeks his own ends and faith which seeks God's. Having said this, however, it must be emphasized that the Gospel is one of life. S. Paul was speaking from his own experience when he put 'the power of the resurrection' before 'reproducing the pattern of his death'.[10]

It is the power of resurrection that Christ brings to the sufferer, and the growing knowledge and experience of this can lead to a desire to share with him the redemptive suffering by which such life, joy, peace and healing may be brought to others.

A Christian congregation is a body in which each has his own contribution to make. In the context of healing there is much an individual can do beyond helping in a caring capacity; each is responsible to become more and more a channel of life, love and power, not only as a powerful intercessor but as one who is a radiant witness in daily life. Of the Apostles it was said 'They took knowledge of them that they had been with Jesus'.[11] This vocation remains whether or not any Christian lives up to it. It is an ideal at which to aim and those who come closest to it are usually unconscious of the fact; self-consciousness can produce a most undesirable parody of the real thing. A Christ-filled life can give something that is an enormous help to the medical practitioner, in whatever field of work he is engaged, not by what he does so much as by what he is, for he is a bearer of the life, joy, light and peace of Christ in all his contacts, bringing the healing radiance of the contemporary Christ wherever he goes.

This is markedly different from the self-conscious 'do-gooder' who, in ignorance, may do much harm. The Christian will be humble enough to accept the advice and wishes of those who specialize in healing techniques in which he is at best only an amateur. He will not be self-assertive but rather available when needed. It was in this way that Christ worked in the days of the

Gospel. For example, of all the sick at the Pool of Bethesda only one was healed; when his fame as a healer was published he withdrew, but when his help was sought he was always available and, according to records, multitudes came to him and he healed every one of them. At Nazareth only a few believed in him and were healed; it was there that he warned the people of their own failure to respond and told them that he came to bring wholeness to those who would receive him.

The Church throughout the centuries has demonstrated that the secret of being a healing church lies in the depth of her spiritual life, enabling her to witness to the world through congregations or individuals to a living, personal knowledge and communion with the contemporary Christ.

'Let those men of zeal, who think by their preaching and exterior works to convert the world, consider that they would be much more edifying to the Church, and more pleasing to God . . . if they would spend at least one half their time in prayer . . . Certainly they would do more, and with less trouble, by one single good work than by a thousand: because of the merit of their prayer, and the spiritual strength it supplies. To act otherwise is to beat the air, to do little more than nothing, sometimes nothing and occasionally even mischief; for God may give up such persons to vanity, so that they may seem to have done something, when in reality their outward occupations bear no fruit; for it is quite certain that good works cannot be done but in the power of God.'[12]

Christian stewardship is not only a matter of talents, money and material service, there is a stewardship at a deeper level, a spiritual contribution. Much is said today about tithing, and this should include time for prayer. To set aside a tenth of the day (two and a half hours) would require genuine sacrifice for many, and would be wrong or impossible for some; but each may well consider this seriously if he really desires renewal for himself and the Church. A spiritually strong church is the fruit of a spiritually alive congregation, and it is usually found that where this is the case financial and other material needs do not cause undue anxiety. The other twenty-one and a half hours of the day will be greatly enriched in this context if supported also by ejaculatory prayer; for prayer is not inaction but the springboard to effective action. There are those today who in the rush and turmoil of a full-time professional life have been able to achieve this and have experienced its great value.

There died in 1904 a Fellow and theological lecturer of Christ's College, Cambridge of whom it was said: 'His life was great, and will for all time remain great, because it was an inspiration . . . men must sometimes have experienced in his presence the same kind of feeling of some great unseen influence at work as that which the disciples must have experienced in the presence of Christ after he, apart and alone, had watched through the night with God in prayer. For many an hour of his life did Forbes spend like that . . . He knew that he could in this way bring to bear upon a man's life more real effective influence than by any word of direct personal teaching or advice. So did he prove once more that the man of power in the spiritual world is the man of prayer'.[13]

At an Ordination in Winchester Cathedral in 1902, speaking to the ordinands he said:

'You have not simply to come to men as an inspiration, but as a revelation . . . Men generally are agreed that pure and simple materialism is no final solution of life's problems . . . They allow that much may be said in support of the existence of some kind of Divine Being, of some kind of spiritual world. Nor can they withhold their admiration from the life of Jesus . . . but further than this the average man hesitates to go. The resurrection may or may not have been true . . . He hardly sees the importance of it . . . You yourself must be the proof that the resurrection has taken place, that Christ is alive. A man will recognize the folly of thinking of Christ as dead in the tomb, if he sees him alive in you. He will grasp the importance of the resurrection as soon as he is brought face to face with a power in you which he cannot account for – the power of the risen Christ. The average man does not know what Christianity is: you must reveal it to him. You must show him . . . what it can do for a human being. You must give him an opportunity of seeing Christ – not as a distant figure in history . . . but as a human, a divine Person, living, moving, working in you. Live Christ before his eyes.'[14]

The revival of the ministry of healing must grow from within and be the outward expression of this vital inner life within the Church. The Gospel of healing is one of a personal relationship with God, for Christianity is not a creed, a theology or a philosophy, but a person who promised 'I will not leave you orphans; I will come back to you'.[15] Since Pentecost, through the power of his Spirit Christ has always been present. Throughout the world today the work and power of his Spirit is very evident, drawing men back to the life of prayer and experience of God, manifesting his manifold gifts, which include healing, and producing the rich fruits of the Spirit, the greatest of which is love.

To be open to the Spirit, to his power and guidance, is the way to experience the wholeness Christ brings both for individuals and for the healing of the ills of the world.

'Lord God, you sanctify your Church in every race and nation by the mystery of Pentecost. Pour out the gifts of the Holy Spirit on all mankind, and fulfil now in the hearts of your faithful what you accomplished when the Gospel was first preached on earth.'[16]

Chapter notes

1. Acts 17. 6.
2. Luke 7. 28.
3. John 3. 4.
4. 'You in Me and I in you, together we are one undivided person . . . now I Myself am united to you, I who am life', from an ancient homily for Holy Saturday.
5. Matthew 11. 25.
6. John 5. 39, 40.
7. cf. Job ch. 38, 39.
8. Francis Thompson.
9. 'If it be Thy will'.
10. Philippians 3. 10.
11. Acts 4. 18 (A.V.).
12. S. John of the Cross, *Spiritual Canticle*.
13. Forbes Robinson, *College & Ordination Addresses*. Preface.
14. Ibid.
15. John 14. 18.
16. Prayer for Whitsunday in the new Western rite.

Appendix

A   Ante-Nicene evidence

A selection of further passages giving evidence of the victory of Christ by:

(I)   witness in persecution (P)

(II) exorcism and healing (H)

Letter from the Church of Vienne on the persecution at Lyons and Vienne.   (see Eusebius. *History V 1*) (P)

Martyrdom of Polycarp   2. 8. 12–16. (P)

Quadratus.   (see Eusebius. *History IV 3*). (H)

Justin Martyr.   *Apology to the Senate II. 6.* (H); *Dialogue with Trypho the Jew 30. 76.* (H)

Irenaeus.   *Against Heresies II. 6.2; 32.4; III. 5.2.* (H)

Minucius Felix.   *Octavius 27.* (H) *37.* (P)

Tertullian.   *Apology 49.* (P) *23.* (H) *26.* (H); *On the Shows 26. 29.* (H); *On the Soul 3. 27. 57.* (H); *To Scapula 4.* (H); *On Baptism 5.* (H)

Clement of Alexandria. *Stromata IV 8.* (P) *II 11.* (P & H)

Origen.   *Against Celsus I 6, 46, 67.* (H) *II 17.* (P) *II 33.* (H) *III 28, 35, 36, 37.* (H) *VII 4, 17, 67.* (H) *VIII 47, 58, 72.* (H)

Cyprian.   *An Exhortation to Martyrdom 10.* (P) *Epistle 8* (P) *32.1.* (P) *33 2–4.* (P) *34.* (P) *76 2, 6.* (P) *74 10.* (H) *75 15, 16.* (H)
On the Vanity of Idols 7. (H)

(pseudo Cyprian).   *On the Glory of Martyrdom 4, 6, 15.* (P)

Gregory Thaumaturgus. *Discourse on All Saints.* (P); See also introductory note on his surname in Ante-Nicene Library (H)

These references can only be fully appreciated in their theological context, see for example the *Epistle to Diognetus* cited on p. 36, or the writings of Irenaeus.

B The Council of Trent 1545–1563

At this Council the scriptural authority for Unction was found in Mark 6. 13 supported by *James* 5. 14–16. Both these passages refer to ministry to the sick irrespective of whether or not the sufferer was near to death; opinion in the Council was strongly divided on the subject of restricting Unction to those in danger of death. This discussion came to an abrupt close with the sudden ending of the first session in 1547 and when the Council reassembled in 1551 the subject was only briefly dealt with. The result was the promulgation of four canons worded in a way which it was hoped would clear up differences of interpretation, misunderstandings and irregularities of practice.

Extreme Unction was described as a sacrament, instituted by Christ and taught by S. James, representing the grace of the Holy Spirit cleansing venial sin and comforting the infirm. The statement says the sick man 'sometimes obtains bodily health when it is expedient for the welfare of his soul'. The second canon omits the word 'Extreme' and anathematizes those who deny its power; the text reads: 'Si quis dixerit sacram infirmorum unctionem non conferre gratiam, nec remittere peccata, nec alleviare infirmos, sed iam cessare, quasi olim tantum fuerit gratia curationum. anathema sit'.

The report of the Council's Commission on this subject noted that physical healing was given more frequently in the Early Church than in the sixteenth century and two reasons for this were adduced, namely, that then it was for the confirmation of the Faith in a pagan world, and as a sign of the healing of the soul.

The Council claimed that nothing in the practice of Extreme Unction was opposed to the teaching of S. James, and interpreted his words 'elders of the church' as meaning episcopally ordained priests.

The divergence of opinion seen in the Council centred upon the word 'Extreme'. What at this stage was meant? Some light is thrown by the discussion as to whether this sacrament could be repeated. Some wanted to wait until the patient was unconscious or actually dead, others would not wait for any danger signal of death. The result was to steer a middle course, the illness must be grave but need not be beyond hope of recovery. Permission for the Sacrament to be repeated was to be given in certain circumstances, namely, if after recovery there was fresh danger of death or if a different disease was in question.[1]

The recognition of Unction as a Sacrament led to the question of age limit. It could not be administered to children who had not yet reached years of discretion. In the sixteenth century the general practice was to fix this age at sixteen but others put it at eighteen, later it was lowered to include younger children on condition that they had received the Eucharist. It subsequently became customary in the West to fix the age limit at seven. In the East there is no limit. For younger children the West provided a rite for blessing and healing with the Laying on of Hands preceded by three very beautiful prayers.

Chapter note

1. See *Summa* 33a.2.4, 9.

C The Eastern Church

Anointing

The one historic recognized form of ministration to the sick in the East is Holy Anointing, and this is very widely used. The alternative title given to the Office for Holy Unction is The Order for the Visitation of the Sick.

In the current English translation of the Orthodox Service Book the following description is given:

'Anointing with the holy oil is a sacrament in which, through the anointing of the body, the grace of God is invoked upon the sick person; because the grace heals all ills, both those of the soul and those of the body. It is performed only over sick persons with one exception: in the cathedral . . . in Moscow on Holy Thursday, the bishop anoints all persons who desire it, after the Divine Liturgy . . . the warrant for this is the saying of S. James taken in its broadest sense to include those who suffer from spiritual ills – grief, despondency, and the like – as well as for those of the body.'

The full office is a very long one requiring seven priests. There are seven Epistles and Gospels, the one to be anointed is anointed in seven places[1] by each one of the priests in turn, each of them saying a long prayer for the sufferer in addition to the prayer used by each during the anointing. Towards the end the priests standing round the one who has been anointed place the Book of the Gospels face downwards on his head – all touching it – symbolic of the hope that he will receive like healing to that recorded in the Gospels, and in order to strengthen his faith in the written word of Christ. The number seven is symbolic of the seven gifts of the Holy Spirit, seven candles are lighted round the vessel containing the oil, and candles are also held by those present.

The origin of this, from monasteries or colleges of priests, accounts for the long ceremonial and the large number of priests; it may be simplified as necessary and performed by a lesser number of priests, usually 5, 3 or 1. When performed by the parish priest there is usually only one Gospel.

The oil (either oil only or oil and wine) is blessed as required by the parish priest and there are no age limits as in the West; even infants may receive it. Except for the general anointing in Holy Week and for infants under the age of seven, the Sacrament of Penance is required beforehand.

The Holy Week general anointing, at which the full office with all seven Gospels, etc.: is used, originated during the siege of Sebastopol (1852–1853) when the bishop offered to all those in danger of death for their lives and souls this sacramental means of repentance and healing. Thence it spread to Moscow and elsewhere, and later became almost general amongst emigrants abroad as a result of the Revolution in Russia, which brought home to them the precarious nature of life and the importance of sacraments.

In Russia at present both this and the sacrament of anointing the sick are restricted; the numbers of believers, the shortage of priests, the difficulty for a priest to go to certain private homes and the ban on his ministry in hospitals all limit individual ministration.

Sick Communion

The Bread is consecrated once a year, on Maundy Thursday – intincted there and then – and kept the whole year in the Tabernacle. A rubric provides for a hot brick to be placed on the altar for drying this after intinction, but this is not always done as it dries of itself and keeps perfectly.

Icons

There are very few Staretzi in Russia today so the faithful are unable to turn to them for help as in the past, but still the peasants can light their votive candles before some icon – and thus ask for the prayers of the saint so venerated. There are a number of icons both on Mount Athos and in Greece and Russia known as healing icons, and certain saints are associated particularly with healing. These include Ss. Pantelemon, Photius and Anikita, Cosmos and Damian, Tinos, and of recent years S. John the Russian whose shrine is on the Greek island of Evvoia.

Exorcism

There is no reference to it in the ordination to minor orders. It is only practised by bishops and priests. The baptismal exorcisms are still used, apart from that it is a matter left to the discretion of individual priests, some of whom practice it frequently, others hardly at all.[2]

Notes

1. Brows, nostrils, cheeks, lips, breast, both sides of hands.
2. See the article 'Exorcism in the Orthodox Church' by Archimandrite Barnabas published in the *Orthodox Observer*, No 51 Spring 1972.

Suggestions for further reading

Melinsky, M. A. H. *Healing Miracles*. Oxford: Mowbrays, 1968.

Lambourne, *Community, Church and Healing*. London: Darton, Longman & Todd, 1963.

Kelsey, M. T. *Healing and Christianity*. London: SCM Press, 1973.

Gusmer, E. W. *The Ministry of Healing in the Church of England*. Great Wakering: Mayhew-McCrimmon, 1975.

Boros, L. *Pain and Providence*. Tunbridge Wells: Burns & Oates, 1966.

Bennet, G. *Commissioned to Heal*. Evesham: Arthur James, 1979.

——*In His Healing Steps*. Evesham: Arthur James 1976.

——*The Heart of Healing*. Evesham: Arthur James, 1971.

Petitpierre, Dom R. *Exorcising Devils*. London: Robert Hale, 1976.

Richards, J. *But deliver us from Evil*. London: Darton, Longman & Todd, 1974.

For a more scientific approach (psychological, medical etc.)

Sandford, A. *The Healing Light*. Evesham: Arthur James, 18th Edition.

——*Healing Gifts of the Spirit*. Evesham: Arthur James, 4th Edition.

Wilson, M. *Health is for People*. London: Darton, Longman & Todd, 1975.

Trowell, H. *Diseases of Strain and Stress*. London: Institute of Religion and Medicine, 1970.

Papers by Members of the Institute of Religion and Medicine under the general title *Religion and Medicine*. **No. 1** 1970, **No. 2** 1973, both edited by Melinsky, M. A. H., and **No. 3**, 1976, edited by Millard, D. W. All three volumes were published by SCM Press (London). The Institute of Religion and Medicine was founded in 1964. Under the same title are papers by members of the Methodist Society for Medical and Pastoral Psychology, edited by John Crowelsmith, and published by Epworth Press (London) in 1962.

Books on more general theology which include valuable insights:

A New Catechism. (The '*Dutch Catechism*') (Especially sections on miracles

Christ and Wholeness

and on suffering) New York: Herder & Herder, 1965. Supplement 1969.

Suenens, Cardinal L. J. *The New Pentecost*. (Especially in reference to suffering) London: Darton, Longman & Todd.

McCabe, H. *The New Creation*. (See chapter on Anointing.) London: Sheed and Ward, 1964. 3rd impression, 1967.

Macquarrie, J. *Principles of Christian Theology*. London: SCM Press, 1966.

Taylor, J. V., *The Go-between God*. London: SCM Press 1972.

For looking ahead, see Chapters 7 and 8.

The Church in the Modern World. An encyclical of Vatican II.

Wall, B. *Heading into Change*. Harekill Press, 1967.

Bliss, K. *The Future of Religion*. London: Watts, 1969.

See also footnotes to pp. 67, 78, 81, 100.